What Do Firefighters Do When There Isn't a Fire !!

Kenneth Wheatley

Published by New Generation Publishing in 2021

Copyright © Kenneth Wheatley 2021

First Edition

The author asserts the moral right under the Copyright, Designs and Patents Act 1988 to be identified as the author of this work.

All Rights reserved. No part of this publication may be reproduced, stored in a retrieval system or transmitted, in any form or by any means without the prior consent of the author, nor be otherwise circulated in any form of binding or cover other than that which it is published and without a similar condition being imposed on the subsequent purchaser.

ISBN 978-1-80031-215-9

www.newgeneration-publishing.com

New Generation Publishing

List of stories

FOREWORD 1

DUFFY AND HIS 'ONE GIANT STEP FOR MANKIND' 10

A GHOST IN THE 'APPY' 13

DES`S TWO-TONE CAR 18

HE WON'T COME OUT OF THE TOILET 'GUV' 21

DES`S NIGHTMARE... 26

CAN WE HAVE OUR BALL BACK, PLEASE 31

WILL HE STILL BE ABLE TO PLAY THE PIANO? .. 34

THE BRAIN DRAIN OR SHOULD THAT BE BRAINLESS DRAIN?.. 39

THE PHANTOM HORSES 43

AMSTERDAM (1)... 49

AMSTERDAM (2)... 56

WHERE IS MICK?... 60

FIREMEN FROM MARS... 63

TAKEN FOR A RIDE 68

DIDN'T SEE ANYTHING OFFICER 72

TRIP TO SPAIN 77

THE EUSTON SPIDER 84

GRATITUDE 87

A NASTY SMELL IN THE TOILET 89

GUARD DUTY 94

LURCH'S CHEESE SANDWICH 98
'THE PHANTOM' 101
THE RETRIBUTER 108
ALL SORTS 114

List of illustrations

1. Future Fireman
2. 17 year old A.F.S. Fireman
3. Squad photo on joining the London Fire Brigade
4. The White Watch Kensington (I'm extreme left)
5. Waiting to take my crew into a fire in Harrods
6. As an instructor at the Brigade's Training school
7. A fire just behind the Fire Station
8. Receiving my Long service and good conduct medal

Foreword

I was born in St Bartholomew's Hospital in the City of London in January 1947. A real and genuine cockney! I was also back in the hospital six months later with pneumonia. My mother told me that I had spent a couple of weeks in an oxygen tent and it was a bit touch and go.

We lived in a rat and bug infested two room flat next to St John's Gate in Clerkenwell with an outside toilet which five families shared. No electricity, just a gas light and fireplace that hardly ever had a fire in it. It was my luck to have been born during the coldest January that century; no wonder I contracted pneumonia.

We eventually moved upmarket to a rat infested and bug ridden three room flat in Shoreditch. It was upmarket because we shared the toilet with only one other family!! The ground floor of this house was derelict and from time to time it was necessary to throw out the odd tramp. The place scared me silly!

Eventually we moved to a council flat near Clerkenwell Fire Station (now closed). Now this flat was really classy, our own toilet and even a bath. I was 11 years of age.

Many think that being born within the sound of Bow Bells applies to the Church in Bow, but in fact it applies to Bow church in the City of London not far from the hospital. Because the Church was in fact bombed during the war, the bells no longer sounded. Thus it came to pass that as long as you were born within 'the sound' of the bells you were a cockney.

Throughout my childhood I played in the derelict and bombed ruins of the City and often spent time at Canon St Fire station just looking at the fire engines and being lucky enough to be shown the engines close up. In fact I became quite friendly with the Firemen.

On the odd occasion I even managed to cadge a lift home from the Firemen on one of their engines as they left the Fire Station (long closed down and replaced by a new station called Dowgate by Southwark Bridge). I lived in Old Street, in Shoreditch, and they would (I now know) have been going to their Divisional Headquarters also in Shoreditch, very close to where I lived, for drills etc. That was my first contact with these people, a contact that was to grow into something inevitable; joining them.

After moving from the rat-infested two rooms in Old Street to council flats in Clerkenwell, I struck up a friendship with another kid called Derek Potts. If anything, he was even more enthusiastic about the Brigade than I was. As Clerkenwell was our local station, we used to hang about outside until they got a 'shout' and followed them as best we could on our pedal bikes. Eventually we expanded our patronage of fire stations and by the time we were about thirteen or fourteen years old were chasing fire engines from Soho, Euston, Clerkenwell and Islington all over London.

By the time I was seventeen I still had this fascination with the Brigade though couldn't join as I had to be eighteen. Derek, who had joined the Auxiliary Fire Service (part time Firemen), suggested that I also join. And so my career as a Fireman began.

After several weeks training, several times a week in the evening, I spent a year with the AFS, stationed at Kingsland Road in the East End of London. I could not get enough of it. The AFS was only part time and most AFS men had full time jobs so it was normal for them to spend maybe one or two evenings a week at the station for three or four hours, with an 'all-nighter' thrown in at the weekend.

I, on the other hand, used to spend three evenings a week and do 'all-nighters' on Friday and Saturday. I did almost more hours at Kingsland Road than I did in my full-time job!

I resolved to join the London Fire Brigade as a 'regular' as soon as I turned eighteen. And when the time came I collected the application forms from Kingsland Fire Station, duly completed and sent them off. Some several weeks passed and I was told to report to the London Fire Brigade Training School in Southwark Bridge Road, S.E.1. for the entrance examination. Proud as a peacock, I turned up and sat the relevant tests which included basic arithmetic, dictation, general knowledge, and a strength test. Finally my chest was measured, and then remeasured after I had inhaled to make sure that I could expand it the required two inches!

Two weeks later the results of my tests came through. I had failed! Apparently my English was just about on a par with that of a Bedouin tribesman and my arithmetic was just about acceptable for a retarded five year old. So much for a comprehensive education! I had a lot of work to do. I worked hard at my three Rs for the next three months and re-applied. This time I made it and was ordered to report to the Training School on the 24th May 1965 at 0830 to commence training as a London Fireman: I had made it!

Because I had no formal qualifications (other than my swimming badge!) I had to train for sixteen weeks. Had I had any educational qualifications such as O or A levels I would have had to train for only twelve weeks. The additional four weeks was taken up not only with arithmetic and English but also continued training in the art of becoming a Fireman. Presumably the powers that be thought that if an individual's ability to calculate and spell correctly was poor then that individual also had trouble climbing ladders or running out hose! Still, I didn't care. They could have flogged me on a daily basis or kept me there for a year. I was in and the devil himself wasn't going to stop me from becoming a Fireman.

The Training School was my first real contact with people who viewed life as I did. It was also my first contact with real and strict discipline. I was a natural. The discipline and training I received at Southwark was to stand me in good stead for the rest of my career and indeed for the rest of my life. I had been a street urchin with occasional brushes with the law and lived my young life almost as I wished. It was also my first introduction into the world of adult tomfoolery. The difference between tomfoolery when you are a child and that when you are an adult is purely a question of degree. As a child, perhaps you threw a cup of water out of a window to wet someone. Now whenever the opportunity presented itself we would turn high-pressure hoses on each other, a potentially dangerous thing to do that did indeed result in several injuries. When lowering our fellow trainees from the fifth or sixth floor of the training tower on the end of a rescue line, it was always worth a giggle to lower the meekest among us at tremendous speed, watching them turn pale or nearly throwing up. I am well aware that in this day of political correctness behaviour such as that is discouraged to such an extent that dismissal would now be a real possibility.

Sometimes there were accidents and on one occasion when we were practising carry-downs a fellow recruit was killed. The pair had just mounted the ladder, paused, and then simply and slowly fell off the ladder. They landed at my feet! My partner and I were supposed to be next to carry out this drill. These days they now use safety equipment that protects the one being carried. In fact, it was that death that brought about the use of a safety device. I would also add that there wasn't any tomfoolery when doing carry downs. We did, however, take pride in how quickly we could descend with someone on our back!

I was always at the front when it came to misbehaving and as such was a target myself. On one occasion, as I was changing out of uniform at the end of the day, I was pounced on by assailants unknown who put a sack over my head, gagged me and trussed me like a turkey. They then lifted me on to the top of the lockers and left me. I couldn't move an inch for I knew where I was and I also knew that it was a long way down to the floor. I stayed like that for nearly seven hours until discovered by a cleaner the next morning! Not a problem for me because my philosophy was always that if I dish it out then I had to be able to take it!!!

The training came to an end and I received my first posting: Kensington White Watch. I was taken to the station by van complete with all my kit. You would be amazed at how much kit a Fireman is issued with. I was given a locker that seemed only to be able to absorb half of what I had and stuffed the rest in the footlocker. As I had been taken to my station on a day my watch were off duty, I went home to await my first day as a real Fireman.

Over the remaining twenty-nine years I transferred to Eltham, Euston and then back to Kensington as a Fireman. At Kensington I was promoted to Leading Fireman and posted to Paddington. From there I was promoted to Sub Officer and posted to Orpington. I managed a transfer back to Euston and from there I was temporarily promoted to Station Officer and posted to the Training Centre as the Brigade's first Physical Training Instructor. Following a spot of bother, I was kicked out of the Training Centre, demoted, and posted to Fulham as Sub Officer.

I managed once again to obtain a transfer back to Euston. From there I was once again temporarily promoted and posted back to the Training Centre, again as a Physical Training Instructor. I was posted and transferred so many times it's a wonder I turned up at the correct station twice on the trot! I transferred eleven times in total as well as several long term temporary postings. I have often wondered if all my transfers had set some sort of Brigade record.

I am one of those lucky few who enjoyed their working lives enormously. The fun and excitement I had over those twenty-nine years will stay with me for the rest of my life. This book is about the funnier and more extrovert side of the Brigade and the things that Firemen get up to when they are not rushing around in a Fire Appliance.

All the stories are perfectly true. It is not meant to show the Brigade in a perfect light but simply the strange and sometimes black humour of a group of men thrown together. The Brigade's professionalism, bravery and dedication to the people of London is a matter of record and in any event others have written about the heroic exploits of Firemen much better than I ever could.

These stories may come as a shock to some but will be of no surprise to those who have belonged to any military or disciplined service that faces danger, serious injury and death on a regular basis. I had a wonderful and fulfilling time as a Fireman and still miss everything about it. The stories have been written using terminology and idiom in use during my time in the service. For example: Fireman; the modern term is now Firefighter to recognise that there are now women employed as Firefighters. I was eventually retired from the Brigade as injuries I had sustained over the years proved too much. I hope that the reader will enjoy these true stories as much as I did in remembering and writing them.

The scruffy kid who used to try and cadge a lift on the Fire Engines when they left Cannon St Fire Station. I'm glad to say I grew into those ears!!

As a 17 year old AFS Fireman (Auxiliary Fire Service). I was still too young to become a professional Fireman so joined the AFS. We rode the famous 'Green Goddesses' and followed the professionals to fires. I spent almost more time on a Fire Station as a part time Fireman than I did as a professional! This photo was taken at Kingsland Road Fire Station.

My squad recruit photo. That's me in the middle back row. 'Lofty' it was and 'Lofty' it remained for the next thirty years!! The two men sitting either side of the instructor fell off the tower that can be seen behind us. One of them died as a result of the fall.

White Watch Kensington lined up for a watch photo for the 'Guv' who was emigrating to Australia. I'm at extreme left, should it need pointing out! That period in the Brigade was the happiest of my whole career. I would have served for nothing. What can't be seen in the photo is the third Fire Appliance to the right. Kensington had three appliances and was a very busy station.

DUFFY AND HIS 'ONE GIANT STEP FOR MANKIND'

Duffy is the surname of a Fireman with whom I served at Kensington on and off for ten years. He came to Kensington as a recruit and we immediately struck up a close friendship. One nutter recognising another nutter I suppose! I was already an old hand, or at least I thought I was, having served all of a year or two before his arrival.

Following drills, there were always several lengths of hose, if not dozens, to be dried. It all depended on the whim of the Officer in Charge (O.I.C.) as to what drills we did and it didn't matter a damn to him how much hose or equipment we used. He wasn't going to have to clean it and re-stow the appliance… On this particular day there were a dozen or so lengths to be hung to dry and Duffy and I were detailed for the job. The drying tower at Kensington is inside the station and is situated in the stairwell running from the basement to the top of the five-storey building. First the wet hose was scrubbed and washed and then it was dragged into the station and lined up so that it would, when hauled, disappear up the stairwell. There were several pulley arrangements designed to accommodate up to twenty lengths of wet hose, usually about three or four lengths per pulley.

Hauling hose is a strength sapping business, which is why it is usually the younger and greener members of the watch who have to do it. Standing in the basement, the two of us would haul away until the ends of the hose were swinging over our heads, drenching us with the water that cascaded from the open couplings. After hauling up several lengths, Duffy decided that the job could be achieved more easily and quickly if, after looping several lengths to the hoist, we went to one of the upper floors and jumped out on to the rope, so allowing our body weight to do the job. Great idea!

Having connected up several lengths of hose to the hoist, we applied the not too exact science of guesstimation, estimating that our combined body weights descending into the basement would haul the hose quickly up the stairwell. A length of wet hose in those days probably weighed about 30 kilograms and we had several attached to the one hoist. We dragged some of the hose into the basement stairwell so that the pulley wouldn't jam and then went to the second floor and peered down into the basement some thirty feet below us. What had seemed a good idea down there suddenly didn't seem so bright from this perspective. I knew Duffy was thinking the same thoughts but since it was his bright idea he couldn't bottle out.

"Right!" he said "When I count to three, we jump. OK?" "Fuck you!" I said. "You jump first and after you have got it moving I will add my weight."

It seemed more logical to me that weight should be applied gradually and not all at once. Having agreed with me, but still not altogether happy with this arrangement, Duffy prepared to launch himself into space. It's worth clarifying at this point that the hoists were of a continuous pulley arrangement. As you pulled the hose up, so the rope came down, you eventually were holding the rope that was at the top at the start of the pull and the hose of course was now at the top. In addition, as there were several pulleys there were also several sets of ropes. As there were several sets of ropes that also gave scope for confusion!

With a cry of bravado, Duffy grabbed a rope and launched himself into the stairwell, hands grasping the hoisting rope in a death- like grip. The one major error of the exercise was that he hadn't first checked that the rope he was now hanging onto with a grip of steel was the right one. In fact, it was the wrong one, and having nothing on the end of the hoist to counter his weight, he disappeared from my view like a bullet out of a gun. Screaming all the way down, his descent into Fire Brigade folklore was arrested by meeting the basement floor with a sickening thump.

It took all of a split second for my brain to work out what had happened and a further split second before my sense of humour clicked in and I started laughing. In fact, I laughed so much I nearly fell down the bloody stairwell too. By the time I was able to get back down to the basement, one or two other Firemen had arrived and were in the process of giving him first aid. I was still laughing like a drain, which really didn't go down too well with anyone. Fortunately Duffy had landed on his back amongst the hose we had dragged into the basement before starting this exercise. Whilst he was unable to move and it took some time before he was again fit for duty, no serious or lasting damage was done. Needless to say, I was never again tempted to try that particular trick and often wonder what would have been the result if we had both jumped out on to that bloody rope as Duffy had suggested we do. There was always scope for an accident when hauling hose up a tower; your hands slipping on a wet pulley or a rope breaking, each of course meaning you ended up with possibly 100kg of wet hose on your head. At least though that is an accident. What Duffy had proposed almost verged on the suicidal! Then again we were just crazy kids and life was a great big ball of fun.

A GHOST IN THE 'APPY'

This next story is about a Fireman who transferred into the London Fire Brigade from the Middlesex Brigade. I was a Fireman at this time and as soon as Don 'Robbo' Robson appeared on the Watch everyone instantly liked him. He immediately became part of the inner sanctum, that is to say that small group of men who for whatever reason became very close. Some might say that this is the definition of a clique, in fact it was said often, but we didn't care a toss. It may have been that I was about nineteen or twenty years of age, as was Don and a few of the others, and that is why we got on so well with each other. We were all 'Jack the Lad' and the older members of the watch tended to treat us like wayward children.

As likeable as Robbo was, he had two failings. He was gullible and he was 'windy'. On many occasions we would be sitting around the mess table on a night shift either playing with a Ouija board or telling stories of ghosts, corpses coming to life etc. You know the normal things that you talk about as an adult holding down a responsible job! Most of this twaddle was for Robbo's benefit. He must have had a great imagination because the end result would be that he would later put his bed as close to another Fireman's as was respectable without causing offence. This was Robbo's way of getting protection should a ghost or hobgoblin creep in and attempt to murder him! And so it came to pass that I decided he should become the victim of a ghost or, in his vivid imagination, something worse!

In those days, the 1970s and 80s, most of the older fire stations' heating and hot water supplies were supplied by a coke boiler usually situated, for obvious reasons, in the lowest part of the building. Kensington, having been built in 1912, was no exception. The boiler, or `appy` as it was known, was situated in the basement at the end of a long and very dark corridor. The word `appy` incidentally comes from the word apparatus or boiler apparatus. I apologise to those of you who knew this, but in my youthful ignorance I assumed that `appy` was in fact its real name and continued believing this for about ten years! Did I really go on to be in charge of a station and thirty men? Ye gods!

At the commencement of a watch, a Fireman was detailed to be the `appy-man`. His job was to ensure that the boiler never went out during the watch and that hot water was in plentiful supply, not only for the station, but also for the Fire Brigade flats above the station. During the day it was a cushy job but when on night duty it was a dirty and time consuming one. Before the `appy-man` went to sleep for the night he had to put the boiler to bed. This involved raking out the slag and setting the damper to a low level so that the boiler burned slowly through the night without any attention. Woe betide any Fireman who let the boiler go out!

On this particular night shift, Robbo was detailed as the `appy-man` which didn`t make him very `appy` at all. He didn`t like the idea of going down into this dark and creepy basement for about half an hour at midnight to bugger about with a boiler that nearly always managed to asphyxiate its attendant. Should you have ever have had the pleasure of raking out a boiler in an airless basement, you will know what I`m talking about. The final part of settling the boiler down for the night was to put your arm through a hole in the wall just above the boiler to partially shut down the damper. This had the effect of slowing the rate at which the coke burned and so hopefully the fire would burn all night. The stage was thus set to get Robbo.

The boiler really was dual purpose, in that it not only supplied hot water to the station but also acted as the heat source for the drying racks built into an enclosed and quite large space behind it. The drying racks were for wet uniforms, and the drying area was accessed by entering another room in the basement. These sliding racks were about two metres high and ran into the drying chamber for about three metres. In all there were about ten of these racks side by side. The rear of the boiler protruded into this area and the effect was to turn it into an airing cupboard but of gargantuan proportions and about five times as hot. In fact, the temperature used to get so high that the plastic leggings some Firemen put in to dry would melt! The hole that Robbo was going to have to put his hand into in order to close down the damper on the boiler led into this drying rack area.

As midnight approached, I sauntered out of the mess room where Robbo and a few of the other others were playing cards and ran down to the basement to set up the wheeze. I hadn't told anyone what I was going to do, as the likelihood would have been that whilst I was preparing to get Robbo they would have quickly organized themselves to pull some nasty stunt on me. The first thing I did was to remove the only light bulb that illuminated the basement corridor. This had the effect of making an already forbidding basement into one that was most definitely creepy. The flickering of the boiler flames at the end of the corridor threw shadows that I knew would make `Robbo cringe. It was also deathly quiet. In fact, it would have made a fine set for a Hammer House of Horror film.

Next I had to insert myself into the drying room. I pulled open a door and the blast of heat that greeted me made me wonder if this was going to be a good idea. As I hadn't told anybody where I was going, I was taking a risk of not only being asphyxiated but done to a turn into the bargain! It crossed my mind that if I passed out in there it wouldn't be until I was smelling pretty ripe that I would be found! I crawled onto the racks and worked my way to the back of the room where the boiler protruded into the drying room. I wedged myself immediately above the boiler, lying prone on a drying rack, and settled down as best I could to wait for Robbo to come down and put the boiler to bed. I was hoping, for the first time in my career, that we wouldn't get a `shout` (a fire call). It seemed to take a long time before I heard the tread of footsteps coming down the stairs and along the corridor. There was a pause, during which time I heard the light switch being toggled. Of course it didn't work, and for a moment I thought that Don's fear of the dark would get the better of him and that he would go and get another bulb. I had judged him right though; his fear of being ridiculed by his mates was greater than his fear of the dark and he stayed.

Don started to whistle loudly as he walked slowly down the corridor. What he was trying to do was frighten away any ghosties that would be lurking in the basement. Like everyone, he knew of course that making some sort of noise would frighten off hobgoblins. The dipstick! I knew that he would already be as frightened as hell and that thought gave me an extremely perverse sense of enjoyment because I knew what was going to happen. Whilst Don went about raking and stoking the boiler I was desperately trying not to giggle or move. My anticipation of what was about to happen almost made me wet myself.

He eventually finished servicing the boiler and, as I have said, the very last thing to be done is to put your hand through the small opening in the wall that gives access to the damper in order to close it down. Knowing that this is the final operation, I had been busy spitting on my hand to make it suitably slimy and clammy. I was fit to burst at this point, and how I kept control of myself was a miracle of self-discipline. Robbo, in a hurry now to get out of the basement, stuck his hand through the opening and the moment I had been waiting for had arrived. With my hand all slimy, I reached out and grabbed his wrist. The result was better than I had anticipated. He let out a howl of absolute and abject terror, trying to drag his hand back out through the opening whilst I held on for grim death, all the while not uttering a sound. His screams were reaching a fantastic crescendo as were his efforts to pull me through a six inch by six inch opening. I held on desperately to his wrist whilst at the same time I equally desperately held on with the other hand so as not to be pulled on to the boiler and badly burned. Eventually I had to let go and Robbo ran off down the corridor shouting and screaming. Hearing him howling his way out of the basement, I nearly came to grief myself. I was laughing so much I nearly fell on to the bloody boiler. As it was I had minor burns and was half-dead from spending the best part of an hour over a furnace.

Of course a joke is only a success if as many people as possible can enjoy it. I knew the rest of the Watch would love this one. I entered the mess to find Don sitting amongst the rest of the watch holding his wrist and looking decidedly uncomfortable. After coming down from whatever planet he had been circling on in his fear, it dawned on him that he had been the victim of a wheeze. Most of the other Firemen were sitting looking at him in an odd and quizzical sort of way which, as I found out, was because he had come flying back into the mess and had sat down without saying a word whilst looking obviously shaken. His hand and wrist were black and blue and oozing blood. As I was the only one missing, he had started to add two and two together and to come up with my name. This was confirmed when I came bursting in sweating and filthy dirty to tell everyone what had happened and further revel in his discomfort. It was a huge success and the watch were merciless in their ribbing.

Robbo claimed that he screamed because he had cut his wrist (which he had) when he tried to pull back out of the boiler, but everyone knew that he had almost had a heart attack. In any event, why had he not turned on his tormentor when he had the opportunity? He would have had me trapped in the drying rack. That was the only part of my plan I had been concerned about. Had that particular wheeze happened to me, I would have locked the bastard in and let him fry. Robbo, to his credit, kept his sense of humour, but the story of his being caught by the ghost in the `appy` will live with him always.

DES`S TWO-TONE CAR

Des, whose brother once said of him "If breathing wasn't automatic he would suffocate because he is so bloody idle". In fact Des probably wasn't any lazier than the rest of us but once a bit of mud is thrown, it does tend to stick. Anyway, here we are at Kensington Fire Station and Des is a member of the Watch. Because Des was doing a bit of part-time work on the side (See Des`s Nightmare!) he was one of the few on the watch who could actually afford a car. I use the term loosely as the car in question was a Hillman Californian of dubious vintage. None the less it was a car and it was Des`s pride and joy, well sort of!

The car was a two-tone brown affair with the upper half being a medium to light brown and the lower half a dark chocolate. At least that was the nearest we could get to establishing the colours because, as I said, he was a lazy bugger and never cleaned it. In fact, in all the years I knew Des he never cleaned a car once. We used to rib him mercilessly about the state of his car but he just used to smile and ignore the remarks. The inside of his car was, if anything, worse than the outside, full of sweet wrappers, fag ends and other rubbish about a foot deep. Whenever someone had the courage to cadge a lift from him they invariably got out of the car somewhat dirtier than when they got in. His answer to any sort of criticism about the state of the car would be "Well, get a fucking bus". Fair enough I suppose!

It was Jock`s idea to pull a wheeze on Des, or rather on his car. As usual this was hatched around the mess table. In those days we didn`t drill or have lectures etc. on Saturday afternoons or Sundays and were left more or less to ourselves. (Obviously emergency calls were dealt with in the normal fashion). We waited until Des was ensconced in his usual position of repose, i.e. in front of the television with his feet up with a fag lit. We knew that, apart from fire calls, he would be there until he could drag himself to his locker to get changed and go off duty. It was a lovely hot day and four of us went downstairs to implement Jock's plan! We couldn't have picked a better day as the heat had baked the car beautifully and the dirt was rock hard all over it. Out came the 'T Cut' (a very effective paint cleaner that removes a fine layer of paint to give that 'showroom finish') and we went to work.

We didn't bother washing the car as we didn't intend to do more work than was necessary to piss Des off. Not only that, but the car being filthy dirty would only improve what we were about to do. The instructions that are clearly written on the tin of 'T Cut' specifically state that whatever the cleaner is used on should be thoroughly washed or damage will definitely occur! We figured Des's car didn't warrant such consideration, what damage can you do to a rubbish skip on wheels? Anyway, the combined effect of both dirt and T Cut were to have an amazingly abrasive effect on the paintwork and achieve spectacular results. It only took about twenty minutes for the four of us to do the complete car. Did I mention that we did the car down the middle from back to front? It was fantastic! We now had a brown four-tone Hillman Californian that was drawing all sorts of looks from the rich and idle who frequent the streets of Kensington on a Saturday afternoon. At least it cleared up one or two misconceptions these people had about what their Firemen are doing when not putting out fires. We thought it was superb. The original two-tone bottom and top was now, of course, divided along its length by another two tones. It looked somewhat like a huge Battenberg cake on wheels. A work of art, we were sure Des would see the funny side of it!

At the change of watch we were all hidden at various vantage points to see his reaction when he went to his car. Down he came and there was a slight pause as he took in the new paint job. His face darkened with anger and we could see that he was most definitely not amused. So much the better! Not much fun if the recipient actually enjoys the wheeze. He took a quick look around, realising he had been had, or rather his car had been had and, seeing lots of grinning faces, jumped in the `Battenberg` and drove off. The only comments we could draw from him over the next few weeks always seemed to include words and expletives along the lines of "children", "stupid bastards" etc. The real joy for us though, was that he lived up to his reputation of being idle and never attempted to clean the car or tone down the `Battenberg` effect. Des continued to drive the car in this state until the engine eventually gave up the ghost as well (lack of maintenance of course) and off it went to the breaker's yard. He made sure the next car he acquired was all one colour!

HE WON'T COME OUT OF THE TOILET 'GUV'

Another boring night shift. Firemen live on other people's misery; it's a simple fact of life. Every time the 'bells go down' some poor sod is in trouble, but to a Fireman the sound of the bells is sweet music indeed. Fires, carnage on the roads, suicides; imagine something terrible and the Fire Brigade is called. The problem for us is that when the populace are behaving themselves a Fireman's job can be quite tedious. Drilling and having lectures only goes so far and it's not long before we start making our own entertainment!

We had just received a new recruit from training school. I had taken an instant dislike to him in any event and would have nothing to do with him. It was strange that I had taken such a stance and it was totally out of character for me but, I just didn't like him. He was an ex-Royal Marine but he certainly wasn't my idea of someone who had been part of that elite military organisation. I knew plenty of ex-military men and they all had a quality, which is a little hard to define but none the less is there. This character moaned a lot and seemed sly; not qualities one associates with the Royal Marines.

As a result of my dislike for him I never missed an opportunity to have a 'dig' at him and this resulted in me nearly breaking his neck on one occasion. There were three of us on top of one of the appliances (Fire engines) cleaning the metal work on the ladders. I had been making sarcastic remarks and generally taking the piss out of him all morning when he decided enough was enough and grabbed me from behind around the neck and proceeded to throttle me! I was sitting with my legs dangling over the back of the appliance and was unable to offer much in the way of resistance. I was so enraged at being attacked from behind that I reacted quickly and violently. I reached back behind me and grabbed his head and neck squeezing and probing in any orifice I could get my fingers into. The pressure on my neck eased somewhat but he wasn't prepared to let go. As I was still slowly being throttled I realised I had to do something quickly as I was close to blacking out! I simply leaned forward and yanked him over my head and off the top of the appliance. It must have been about ten feet or so to the ground and he hit a few things on the way down as well. He was fortunate not to have been badly injured but was sufficiently battered and bruised to remain 'off the run' for the rest of the shift. I would have been quite happy to have continued the affair but a couple of the others calmed the situation and did point out that it was all my fault anyway! As I couldn't really argue that point I simply shrugged and got on, rather sulkily, with my work. But from then on he avoided me like the plague.

It was during the following nightshift that once again we were doomed to cross 'swords'! I had been watching television until around 11.30 and after closing it down wandered into the locker room to try and get some sleep, always difficult for me. When I entered the locker room, sitting on one of the cots already made up, were a couple of Fireman who really were co-conspirators to any madcap scheme that was going, plus my ex Royal Marine!

I immediately looked at my watch and said "o.k., let's do it at midnight" I didn't really have a clue what I was talking about but felt the ex Royal would get hold of the wrong end of the stick and assume it was something we were going to do to him at midnight! The other two, equally didn't have a clue what I was talking about but simply went along with the comment. In fact, I intended to get some sleep at midnight!

As the time passed by my comments about midnight approaching and that something was going to happen became more 'threatening' Not once did I refer to the ex-Marine but simply let him think it was something to do with him. As I have said, I was going to bed at midnight.

As the 'bewitching' hour approached he became more and more agitated and demanded to know what we were going to do at midnight. I simply said, "you will find out" With just a few minutes to go he suddenly upped and rushed out to the toilet locking himself in. Having thought that was the end of it I said to the others we might as well try and get some sleep, as it wasn't often we got through a night shift without several calls. With that we all 'turned in' without a thought of the man in the toilet!

I must have drifted off to sleep as it was around 3 o'clock in the morning that Des, one of the other Fireman who had been sitting on the cot talking, woke me and told me that the ex-Marine was still in the toilet! Des had got up to visit the loo and discovered him still locked in there. He had tried to talk him out, but he wouldn't have none of it claiming that Des was part of the conspiracy and simply wanted to get him out of the toilet so we could do to him whatever he thought it was we were going to do!

By now several other members of the watch were awake and taking an interest in what was going on. The more responsible and older Firemen thought it had all gone far enough and a couple tried to talk him out of the toilet, to no avail, he simply wouldn't come out and claimed they were all part of the same conspiracy. It was pointed out to him that he couldn't, in any event, stay in the toilet forever and would have to come out some time. He mulled that little gem over for a minute or two then said he would only come out if the Officer in Charge was present.

As I was the one who had started the whole thing I was elected to go and wake up the 'old man' not something to take lightly as he wasn't the most patient of men and considered practical jokes to be stupid and discouraged. However, into his room I went, and after waking him explained that he had a Fireman, who had locked himself in the toilet, had been there for hours and won't come out.

He warned me that if this was a joke, he would have my head on a plate. He probably would have too, he was that sort of man; an ex merchant Navy stoker who had survived the Russian convoys during the war. Not a man to bugger about with! I assured him it was true and so we made our way back to the toilets.

By now most of the watch had gathered around the toilets and the comments were coming thick and fast. I thought the best one was that the reason he had been in there most of the night was because he was constipated! Fireman are not particularly noted for their compassion in such circumstances!

The 'boss' rapped on the toilet door and told the hapless man to come out. In reply the aforementioned hapless man promptly accused the Station officer of being part of the conspiracy! Hearing that everyone near collapsed with laughter, the 'boss' realising that this was perhaps somewhat more serious suggested that the man talk to him through the toilet window, which opened on to a flat roof. So now we had the comical situation (in our view!) of the Officer in Charge of a fire station standing in freezing temperatures talking to a Fireman through the toilet window and trying to convince him to come out of the toilet as there was no conspiracy and it was all in his mind.

The Fireman flatly refused, again, accusing the Officer of being part of the 'conspiracy'. It took a lot of patience on the part of the 'the boss' but eventually he did talk him out. It was to our great delight that the way he finally managed it was to promise the man that he could sleep with him in his room and that he would be protected! We loved it!

Eventually we all settled down, making all sorts of smart and ribald remarks and thought that that was the end of it. A postscript though was that as soon as morning came the Fireman went off duty never to return. He resigned that very day and nothing was ever heard of him again.

The reader may judge that in these days of political correctness, anti-bullying atmosphere and 'the weak shall prosper' attitude that what happened that night was grossly unfair. The reader may indeed be right but, to keep a perspective, most of those involved were very young Fireman; (I was only 18 years of age) and to a 'man' we had all been reared in a fairly tough upbringing. The Fire Brigade then was full of ex-servicemen and youngsters like me who had little compassion for those who showed weakness. Not right, but that was the reality at the time. Attitudes and behaviour were different back then and I still think, better!!! The reader may well disagree!

DES`S NIGHTMARE

This little tale is about one of the men I worked with at Kensington Fire Station and his part-time job that was responsible for frightening the life out of everyone on a night shift.

Des had been at Kensington for about a year when he was asked by one of the older hands if he would like to do a bit of part-time work. Like most young men, Des was footloose and fancy-free and could always use extra few bob, particularly a few tax free bob, so he said yes. In itself that was a surprise since Des was, not to put it too diplomatically, a lazy bastard, but that is another story! 'Shiner', the aforesaid older hand, told Des that unlike most part time work his future work required that he turn up looking tiddly in a dark suit and black tie. We all knew that Shiner ran the local undertakers' office in Kensington and was looking for a new assistant. He had been doing it for years and looked as if he had too! Most of us had been approached by Shiner in the past, but none of us had really fancied working that close to 'stiffs'. We usually saw enough of that side of things in our daily work and didn't fancy handling them off duty as well. Des probably thought he was going to be a waiter or something. As he was a dark, sombre-looking type, he fitted the role perfectly, but what he didn't appreciate was that he was going to be handling bodies that were in all sorts of condition in a sort of cheek by jowl situation.

He duly reported for work at the Undertakers where Shiner delighted in introducing him to the finer points of making a decomposing body presentable for viewing and burial. Shiner had been doing the work most of his life and had absolutely no problems with it. Indeed he was one of the most callous men I was ever to meet in the Brigade. When Des reported for duty on our next shift we couldn't get a single word out of him about his new job. In fact, he appeared to be slightly traumatised by his experiences. Shiner took great delight in filling us in on all the gory details surrounding Des's first couple of days at the undertakers. We could now appreciate why Des was more than somewhat reticent to discuss his part-time work. It is a particularly difficult job and not everyone is cut out for it. Des certainly wasn't! If you have ever watched a popular fictional television programme about the London Fire Brigade you will have realised that just about every Fireman has a nickname. For some unaccountable reason, Des's became 'The Devil's Apprentice'. (Mine was Lofty - being 6ft 6ins might have had something to do with it!)

Des had now been working at the undertakers for a couple of months and, whilst we had more or less stopped making wisecracks at his expense, what we delighted in calling his 'trauma' hadn't gone. In fact, it seemed worse. It was on a subsequent night shift that it all eventually came to a head when one of the stiffs he had been working on during the day came to 'visit' him! The earlier part of the night shift had been carried out as normal and now approaching midnight we were free to get our heads down if we wished. Kensington was a busy station and it was normal to have five or six 'shouts' (emergency calls) a night so it was prudent to try and get some sleep in between. The locker room also served as the dormitory and had lockers around the walls and down the centre, forming an island. The Firemen arranged their cots around this island and as many as six or seven would attempt to get some sleep amid the snoring, burping and farting. Sometimes it was akin to trying to sleep at the London Zoo. Des, along with two other Firemen, was sleeping on one side of the island, whilst another Fireman and I were sleeping on the other side.

Any large room or building can be quite creepy. Fire stations, I always found, are very creepy places. Kensington with its history of Firemen killed on duty and being the last station to have had horses to pull its engines was no exception. It was in the early hours of the morning and even Kensington goes quiet in the middle of the night. The locker room was deathly quiet. Some of the men were, like me, just dozing that halfway stage between sleep and wakefulness. Throughout my career I always found it difficult to sleep on a Fire Station. The thought, as so often the thought became the reality, of shifting from the state of relaxation to one of intense activity in a split second responding to the alarm, never allowed me to sleep properly. Des was having no such problems. He was fast asleep, or at least appeared to be.

The scream that pierced the deathly silence was so frightening and so long that when it eventually stopped not a soul dared move or say anything. Everyone was aware that the others were awake yet our nerves were so bloody jangled by that horrendous scream that nobody budged. A second piercing scream, followed by gurgling and a strange sobbing, sent my heart rate through the roof. I'm not the bravest man ever to be employed by the London Fire Brigade and like everyone else I didn't want to move or bring attention to myself in case I became the subject of some frenzied attack. However, somebody had to get out of bed and switch the lights on, and as I was the nearest, I flew at the switch and turned them on. Everybody knows it's only in the dark that nasty things happen so the relief was quite palpable on everyone's face. All the men were sitting up on their cots with eyes wide open and a look of apprehension. Everyone that is except one person.

Des too was sitting up in bed but his eyes were glazed and he was drooling and gurgling. He looked dreadful and appeared to be just short of going completely crazy! He was frightening the bloody life out of us. What was really weird was that he was trying to strangle himself! To be exact, his right hand was trying to strangle him whilst his left was trying to pull it away. All this time he was dribbling and muttering like a demented idiot. My racing pulse was now slowing to something like normal. The rest of the lads were also gathering around and it was obvious that our courage was returning by one or two wisecracks that were made.

Des, oblivious to us, still carried on in this fascinating attempt to strangle himself. I had a vague feeling that someone in this sort of state shouldn't be touched but should be allowed to come out of it by themselves. I was right! One of the other lads, now we were all brave again with the lights on, reached down and shook his shoulder. The effect was astonishing. Des let out another blood-curdling scream then lashed out and knocked the Fireman across the locker room. Then he jumped out of his bed and ran screaming around the locker room, bouncing off lockers and still trying to strangle himself like some lunatic who had just escaped from an asylum. Enough was enough. To a man we fought to get out of the locker room and leave Des to either come around or succeed in strangling himself. There is a strange paradox with Fireman that they will take all sorts of risks in an attempt to save life, indeed that's what they are paid for, but when it comes to a situation like this then it's bollocks to that! Particularly if they happen to be frightening the life out of us at the time.

A few minutes went by and things quietened down in the locker room. A couple of the braver ones crept back in, expecting to be assaulted by some maniac wielding a Fireman's axe or confronted by Des lying dead on the ground, having succeeded in strangling himself. Instead there he was, sitting on a locker with his head in his hands and trembling like a gun dog. From a safe distance someone asked if he was OK. He looked up and we could see that he had returned to planet earth. The return looked as if it had been a bad one, so we thought it prudent to continue talking to him from a safe distance. A few minutes passed and we approached him, now of course all caring and solicitude personified. It transpired that it had been a nightmare of gargantuan proportions. He had (in this nightmare) been working with Shiner in the mortuary when a corpse lying on an adjacent trolley had started to move. He said that he peered into its face to see if it was alive (bodies do in fact move and make funny noises!) and that as he bent down this particular body reached up and grabbed him by the throat, and proceeded to throttle him. Grabbing his own throat of course reinforced the nightmare. He also said that he remembered someone touching his shoulder and thought another corpse was grabbing him from behind. That is what sent him from having a bad nightmare into bloody orbit.

For months afterwards when we were on nights and trying to get some sleep there would be some silly bugger hiding under someone's bed ready to grab them as they were falling asleep or someone else making ghostly noises in the middle of the night. All very adult! Des very soon after quit his part-time work. Very wise we all thought, although he remained forever 'The Devil's Apprentice'. I don't think he ever took another part time job again.

CAN WE HAVE OUR BALL BACK, PLEASE

Kensington Fire Station backs on to the Israeli Embassy. There is simply a dividing wall between the two properties; granted it was about twenty feet high but that never proved to be much of an obstacle to us when our football went over and into the Israeli gardens.

The 'Guvnor', 'Darby' Allen was a fitness fanatic and his favorite fitness training sessions were a sort of game of football! I say 'a sort of' because other than a ball and kicking it, the resemblance to football ends. Physical contact was very much a part of the game and when in possession of the ball it was necessary to keep a very sharp lookout as you were as liable to be charged in the back, kicked and even sometimes punched!!

I entered into the spirit of this type of football as soon as I arrived on the station. I had been posted there straight from Training School where I had passed out as a recruit. In fact, I entered into it with so much enthusiasm that on my second day on duty I had to go to the Hospital where an x-ray showed I had broken a bone in my foot!! As a result I was off sick for several weeks whilst it healed!!

The semi-official fitness training sanctioned by the Brigade was, in fact, volleyball but 'Darby' considered that sport to be too 'wimpish' and so his version of football was the one we mainly played. As perhaps can be imagined the ball would be secondary to the violence, the Eton Wall game was for wimps by comparison.

Often the ball would be flying through the air whilst the players were busy fending for themselves. The ball would, from time to time, end up going over the dividing wall between the Israeli embassy and it was simply a matter of throwing a rope over the wall scaling up and lowering down into their garden; throw the ball back and then reverse the procedure to get back into the Fire Station.

This 'happy' situation continued for several years. I must have climbed that wall countless times and wandered around the embassy gardens looking for our ball. No one seemed to be bothered that we were 'invading' Israeli sovereign territory. I'm sure the embassy staff could see us as there were cameras everywhere. No one ever troubled us though and retrieving the ball continued.

That 'happy' situation was to come to an end though following a spate of letter bomb attacks on the embassy. We actually attended the first letter bomb incident when a secretary was killed opening the letter. Obviously security from that moment was considerably tightened and that included anyone trying to get their ball back!

Some weeks later we were again playing our version of football in the station yard and sure enough over the wall went the ball. "Right Wheatley, over you go and find it." So, once again using a long rope up and over I went and started searching amongst the shrubbery for our ball.

"Stand still" was the first thing I heard as I found the ball and was about to throw it back over the wall. I turned my head and saw two men, tough looking men too, a few yards away but what really grabbed my attention were the guns they carried and were pointing at me!!

"Who are you"? one of them asked and I rather stupidly mumbled back that I was looking for my lost ball! Again, "Who are you?" This time as the initial shock wore off I told them I was a Fireman and that we had kicked our football over the wall and that we always climbed over to retrieve it. "No more" said one of the men and went on to say that I had to leave by the front of the embassy.

"Wheatley, where's that fucking ball" I heard my Guvnor shout. I called back that I couldn't throw it as two men were about to escort me out the front door. "Never mind that, throw the fucking ball back and get over here at once" "Guvnor, I can't do that" "Why?" Cos, they have got guns and they are pointing the fucking things at me!!! Silence!

I was escorted out of the embassy by the two security men and told never, ever climb over that wall again and to make sure no one else ever did. Because of the killing of the secretary security had been ramped up to a very high level and there was now a very real danger of someone being shot if they trespassed in the embassy grounds.

The security men were, of course only doing their job and probably showed great restraint regarding me after listening to my implausible story. After all, who scales a wall into a sovereign embassy to get their football back?

We still played football of course and the ball still, from time to time, went over the wall but the days of scaling the wall were over, literally perhaps on pain of death!! The embassy staff though remained friendly to us and whenever the ball went over the wall a Fireman was sent around to the embassy to ask for it back. Someone from the staff would go out in to the garden and throw it back over the wall.

It seems incredible looking back at those times just how the Israelis allowed us to climb into the embassy. These days I doubt you can even get to the front door of the embassy without being stopped and searched.

WILL HE STILL BE ABLE TO PLAY THE PIANO?

It's difficult to laugh while not so slowly suffocating but that was the situation I found myself in while trying to ventilate a smoke filled room at a fire in a house in Cromwell Road, West London. I found myself teamed up with Robbo (Don Robson). The Guvnor had ordered the two of us to ventilate the ground floor of a house, which was smoke logged, whilst the remainder of the fire crews were fighting a fire in the basement. It was the unglamorous side of firefighting but was also a vital part to prevent unnecessary damage and it helped make life easier for other crews searching for possible victims.

There was always a rush to be at the firefighting head of any attack on a fire, after all that was why we had joined in the first place, not to bugger about letting smoke out but never the less it had to be done and on this particular occasion the job fell to Robbo and me.

Heat and smoke rise, so the fire burning merrily away in the basement was making our job harder by the second and the rooms we were to ventilate were filling with an atmosphere that is lethal after being exposed to it for just a few minutes. We both knew that once we were in a smoke filled room then it was of the very essence that the room be ventilated quickly not only to mitigate damage to furniture and property but to ensure our own survival and I have to admit worrying about some poor sod's furniture and treasured possessions came a very poor second! Often breathing apparatus was used to help men doing this work because by definition it is very difficult to breathe! If it all goes tits up and you become disorientated and lost which is very easy to do, even in a small room, then it is no exaggeration to say you can be dead in a minute or two! In this case the Guvnor considered that using breathing apparatus was a bit 'wimpish' and in addition, he wasn't using his lungs. He had no problem ordering us to get in and ventilate.

The standard and indeed only way you can make any progress in a completely black, sound deadened room whilst desperately trying to filter some oxygen through the hairs up your nose is to lie flat on your stomach and crawl in a fashion that would do credit to a snake, the theory being that there was always a thin layer of breathable air about an inch or so above the ground. In reality I had always considered that theory to be bullshit as I was never in my whole career able to breathe easier whilst scrapping my nose along the ground! It was usually very hot and not a little frightening so negotiating a room full of furniture carefully wasn't really an option and personal belongings and furniture would often just be thrown aside in a desperate quest for the nearest window and survival.

You don't have to have a degree in civil engineering to know that windows are usually placed on the walls of a room and that is where, if you have any survival instincts, you head for once you enter a smoke-filled room. Like a demented homing pigeon a Fireman will scuttle across the floor until he crashes head on into a wall. It is simply then a matter of time until a window is found by crawling along the floor and either reaching up now and again like a drowning man grasping for a lifebelt or seeing a faint glimmer of daylight through a smoke blackened window (knackered of course if the fire is at night).

Once the window has been found then two methods of ventilating the smoke are employed. The first is hardly scientific but does require a certain understanding of how windows are opened, i.e. they usually slide up and down or open horizontally! This is where all that detailed and concentrated lecturing on building construction pays off! Glass also breaks quite easily so the standard practice was in fact hurling something heavy straight through it and to hell with detailed building construction techniques. This second option worked every time! From experience windows were often locked and whilst the owner might appreciate that we had gone to the trouble of looking for the key to unlock the window rather than destroying the window we, the unfortunate, coughing and spluttering Firemen considered such an option as stupid!

Robbo, who had found a window, for reasons he never explained decided that he would forgo the tried and trusted way of opening a window, i.e. smashing it, and proceeded to open it as if he was in his own home casually letting in fresh air instead of being in a smoke-filled room coughing his lungs up! The houses in west London are a mixture of Victorian and Georgian construction and just about every one of them had sash cord windows. For readers reared on double glazing and patio windows these windows are of the type which had to be slid up in a sort of groove either side of the window so that either the bottom half was open or conversely the top half pulled down to let air in at the top.

The size of these windows normally makes it near impossible to open them without the help of a large iron counter weight hidden in the side of the window frame. These weights were attached to the window by a rope or cord, hence the name sash cord windows. The one very big problem with this is that the ropes become rotten and need to be replaced from time to time. If not, then the window just becomes a huge dead weight requiring almost superhuman effort to open it.

Having found the window and now needing air in much the same way as someone who is submerged under water without the benefit of a scuba set needs air, Robbo leapt to his feet, grabbed the lower half of the window and threw it open with a strength born of desperation. He was both fortunate, and as we will come to see, and unfortunate. That the sash cord maybe was broken didn't enter the equation at all and in his desperation for oxygen he had the strength of ten men and the window flew open as if it was as light as a feather instead of something probably weighing 30 kilos or more!

Physics plays an important part in what happened next and Isaac Newton would have been most pleased! With a now gaping space where the window had been fresh air now beckoned. Having lifted the lower half of the window he let it go and placed his hands in one fluid motion on the window sill beneath prior to sticking his head out. The window also in one fluid motion and lacking the counterweight due to a rotten sash cord and also acting in complete agreement with Mr. Newton's laws of gravity descended like an express train and slammed into his hands just as he placed them on the sill. I suppose it was in some way fortunate that his head, following his hands, was still descending and hadn't yet been thrust out into the open!

I watched all of this as if in slow motion and cringed as the window crashed into his hands trapping them completely. Feeling quite relieved they were his hands and not mine I raised myself up on my knees to try and free them. Robbo in the meantime was screaming in agony! The pain must have been excruciating and his fingers had actually taken on the contours of the window frame which was quite remarkable as I half expected them to have been cleanly amputated!

Humour is very subjective and I have to admit that I had to exert great control and not start laughing out loud at what had just happened. It's not that I'm some sort of pervert but rather I saw the funny side of it in the same way as someone watching a cartoon film where the 'Roadrunner' or other character runs into a tree or falls off a cliff.

I couldn't break up the window for fear of injuring 'Robbo' further and arrived at the conclusion that if I didn't get his bloody hands out of the trap in the next few seconds the pair of us would be found by another crew searching for us as we were both coughing and spluttering for want of air!

In utter desperation I prised the jammed window from his hands using an axe and released him. He fell to the floor sobbing with the pain. A split second later I was on the floor beside him and gasping for oxygen, I half dragged him out the way we had come in and I was still chuckling in an almost hysterical fashion. By the time we got out of that room we were both in a quite bad way and as we emerged other crew members came to help, sense of camaraderie and all that!

Robbo's hands were in a quite a bad way, swollen, bleeding and looking as if they had been through a mangle. He was taken to hospital by ambulance where by some miracle none of his fingers were found to be broken, badly mashed up and bent at all sorts of angles, but not broken. Once in the fresh air I recovered quickly and chuckling, recounted the tale, embellishing it of course to make Robbo look as stupid as possible!

It was much to everyone's amusement and the usual jokes followed: will he still be able to play the piano, pick his nose etc.? From start to finish that little episode probably lasted only five or six minutes but seemed, as it always did, like an eternity. 'Robbo' was off sick for quite a long time but eventually returned to duty. Don also had a great sense of humour and we often had a laugh about that particular incident. I'm still bloody glad though that he found that window before I did!!!

THE BRAIN DRAIN OR SHOULD THAT BE BRAINLESS DRAIN?

The Firefighters of today are somewhat spoilt compared to most of my time as a Fireman. Now, if ever there is any sort of problem on a Fire Station then contractors are quickly brought in to sort it. They now have window cleaners, general station cleaners, vehicle contractors and repair men to resolve any problem with the building.

I suppose I should admit that halfway through my career in the service we too had window and station cleaners. At first it seemed a great step forward, no more scrubbing and polishing floors and cleaning windows, great! No doubt many thought so but gradually it dawned on even the laziest of Fireman that stations were becoming grubbier and grubbier. The fact is Firemen looked after their own stations far better than any professional cleaners.

I never had a problem with station cleaning. I took as much pride in polishing the floor to a brilliant shine as I did my Firemanship. Others looked at it differently believing themselves to be above keeping their own living quarters clean and tidy! There is no question in my mind that when the station personnel did the cleaning then stations were cleaner than the average hospital!!

Whenever there was a problem, in the days before contractors were routinely brought in, the first thought was can we fix it? At Kensington we even repainted the whole of the ground floor messrooms because it was felt they were too grubby. Yes, the Officer in Charge could have submitted a report asking for the place to be decorated but the whole process would have taken months and even then probably been refused. So, the Officers on all watches agreed and somehow found the money for the paint and we, the Fireman, did the work. We also got some spare time off as a reward. After all we were not stupid.

It was with this DIY ethos in mind that one day, when it was discovered that a toilet was blocked, we tried to resolve the problem ourselves. It didn't take much imagination to work out why it was blocked. The toilet in question was a suite of two which sat in their own lobby and the toilets were divided by a wall and of course were private with their own doors.

One of the men reported the blockage to the boss who promptly suggested that we clear it ourselves so a couple of us started investigating. First was the inspection hatch that was on the waste down pipe from the toilets on the first floor and continued down the appliance room wall and on through the appliance room floor to the sewer. We took off the inspection hatch, very carefully I might add, bearing in mind what could come out. Nothing, it was as dry as a bone and quite obviously nothing had passed this way for some time, no pun (at this point!) intended.

So, back to the blocked toilet. We decided that there were only two ways to clear a blocked drain and that was either with drain rods or a high-powered jet of water to clear the blockage. Fire stations and fire appliances have a huge and extensive selection of tools and equipment for emergencies as you would expect but definitely not drain cleaning rods. I suppose it was considered that we would never be called, in an emergency, to a blocked toilet.

What we did have, in abundance, was lots of hose and even more 'lots of' high pressure water at our disposal. We connected up several lengths of hose to one of the fire appliances, running the hose up the stairs to the first floor and into the toilet which was blocked. On the end of the hose was of course a branch (a controllable on/off jet). The hose was charged with high pressure water from the fire appliance and we stuck it down the toilet bowl into the murky mess we wanted to clear.

Not without trepidation the branch was opened slowly, after all the last thing we wanted was a 'splash back'. High pressure water was forcing its way down into the toilet and seemed to be working well so the branch was fully opened and the flushing process started to work as the bowl of muck was siphoned away by the high-pressure water.

The noise a high-pressure hose makes when working is considerable and it was a minute or two before we realised that there was a lot of shouting going on. We also realised that our feet were getting quite wet!!! Shutting down the branch we both backed out of the toilet to be confronted with a scene of utter chaos and filth.

What we didn't know was that the two toilets, though separate cubicles with a dividing wall, were joined by a common waste pipe that fed into the down pipe in the appliance room. Whilst we were busy pouring high pressure water down our toilet, because of the blockage, it was just passing between the common waste pipe and blasting out of next door's toilet. There was shit and toilet paper on the ceiling, walls and of course the floor was awash with this stinking mess.

It wasn't until the effluent had run out of the toilet lobby and was now descending the stairs that someone had seen it and that was what all the shouting was about. Looking suitably abashed and not a little stupid we pulled out the hose and started making some effort to clean up. The rest of the watch were none too amused as they had to help.

There is a wonderful and totally true postscript to this story. The reader may recall that when this blockage was first investigated by us we had removed an inspection plate on the downpipe in the appliance room. We had also forgotten to replace it!!

When the furor of our endeavors reached the office where the Station Officer was doing whatever station Officers do, he decided to come and see what all the noise was about. The office was situated just a few yards from the waste downpipe. Being the O.I.C he was always dressed in his 'number 1s', that is to say his uniform of dress jacket, trousers; white shirt and tie. I didn't see what happened next but I did see him a few minutes later so know it to be true. As he walked past the open inspection hatch in the drain pipe the blockage above, probably due to our earlier efforts, broke free, and shot out of the waste pipe at a considerable pressure covering him in crap, brown liquid and toilet paper.

Given that this officer was a fastidious man who was taken to having at least two showers a day, the effect was to send him ballistic. Needless to say, everyone on the watch thought it hilarious, except him! He was absolutely convinced we had done it deliberately but that was never the case, just pure unadulterated coincidence.

It seemed to take forever to clean the mess up and the two of us who were responsible were not too popular for the rest of the day. Eventually the station was as pristine as it was before this episode began and the Guvnor never did accept that it really was an act of God that covered him in crap. Fortunately he couldn't prove otherwise.

THE PHANTOM HORSES

Kensington Fire Station was the last station in the London Fire Brigade to have horses pulling a Fire Engine to fires. It was, if my history is correct, 1912 when the last horses were pensioned off and Kensington became a station full of those very modern petrol things. Probably as a result of having the last horses in the Brigade, there was always a story or two going the rounds about ghost horses that would from time to time make their presence known by ghostly hauntings and loud 'neighing` noises! In actual fact when I served there as a young Fireman I was on the same watch as an old hand who did remember the horses from his youth.

Anyway, I had been at the station for a couple of years when a new Guvnor going by the name of Dizzy Sargeant was posted to us as our new Officer in Charge. He was well named since his cock-ups were both legendary and hilarious. That is not to say he was bad at his job. On the contrary, he was very good at it. He just made a lot of cock-ups! His main problem was that he was nearly blind and without spectacles he was. How he managed to pass the periodical medical examinations nobody could understand. This often led to him speaking to the wrong people and even getting on the wrong fire appliance from time to time. Yes, his vision was that bad! He was shielded from coming to real grief by his Junior Officers and by the Firemen on his watch. Dizzy also loved practical jokes.

The phantom horses started to rear their phantom heads, metaphorically speaking, around the mess table one day when Dizzy asked, quite casually but also very straight-faced and seriously, if anyone had heard the phantom horses during the previous night shift. As always, comments of this sort would bring forth all sorts of unprintable comments and funny remarks. What he was doing, of course, was sowing the seeds for one of his practical jokes. At least we felt sure after the event it was one of his jokes, but.....!

We were a very young watch and one or two of the Firemen were still at that impressionable age where, with enough forceful suggestion, they would believe almost anything. Anyway, Dizzy persisted over a period of months with sowing the seeds of phantom horses galloping around the station in the middle of the night. I'm absolutely sure that more than a couple of the young Firemen by this time had swallowed all his bullshit completely. Or should I say horse shit?

It all came to a head on a night shift, of course. The middle of the night is always best for creepy happenings. One of the impressionable 'bucks' (new Firemen) was the watchroom attendant. His duties involved him having to stay in a room on his own throughout the night to receive any emergency calls we might get from Headquarters and dispatch the appropriate fire appliance. By coincidence, the watchroom where this man was keeping watch had actually been the stables for the horses! There were even the original ringbolts and bits of other ironware still affixed to the walls. Of course the lad was fully aware of the history of Kensington thanks to the persistent story telling of Dizzy.

Now I defy anybody not to have the odd hair stand up on the back of their neck whilst wandering around a fire station on their own in the middle of the night. They are creepy places. Of course no one would ever own up to being frightened but I have seen enough men jump with fright when something strange has occurred. Along with empty ships and derelict buildings, fire stations seem to have a strange and pervasive atmosphere about them. Maybe it is the appliances sitting there in the semi-darkness like big brooding monsters waiting to speed off into the night, with their crew's fire uniforms draped over the doors and seats like collapsed corpses waiting to be filled and come to life. Believe me, a fire station in the dead of night is intimidatingly scary.

This particular night shift was to be the night of 'The Return of The Phantom Horses'. The shift had been pretty uneventful, with just the usual few calls to small fires and the odd car crash. A lecture was followed by some volleyball, then supper and the rest of the evening was our own. Some of the men would play snooker. Others would watch television, wash their kit or study for promotion. Providing you were always ready for instantaneous response to a fire call, you could do almost anything legal!

The shift drifted by. Eventually the watch, as a whole, was asleep or as near as you can get to sleep on a canvas cot. It would normally be about one or two o'clock in the morning before the whole watch bedded down. There was always someone who refused to accept that the last shout was in fact the last one. The expectation of being roused from a somnolent state by the manic clanging of the fire alarm call bells, causing your heart to pound its way out of your chest by the sudden exertion, was almost too much for some to bear, and sleep would be resisted far into the night. Eventually though everyone would succumb and there would be total peace and quiet. Absolute calm.

Let me describe briefly, before I go on, what happens when a fire call is received. When someone dials 999, the operator passes the call to Fire Brigade Headquarters who in turn pass it to the nearest fire station. They do this in the most expedient and unsubtle way imaginable. Imagine the scene, a completely darkened building with any number of men asleep, scattered about in various rooms. Suddenly the whole building and all of the rooms are brightly lit by the call out lights. At exactly the same time, the alarm bells begin their clamour. Each bell is as loud as a single burglar alarm and every room on the station has one of these bloody things in it. The effect on the central nervous system is to galvanize the human body into movement even before the brain puts together any coherent thoughts. Your heart rate has gone from the average 70-80 beats a minute to something approaching 180 or more, all in the space of a few seconds. How I survived thirty years of that, only my cardiologist can tell me.

Anyway back to the story. Absolute calm. Suddenly it's all lights and noise, as the fire call system calls us to our appliances to head out to God knows what. Men stumble about trying to figure out how to get down stairs without breaking their necks. Others use the fire poles and definitely risk breaking their necks. Indeed, many have suffered serious injury just answering the call bells and I know of one death as a result. None the less, the whole watch in a zombie-like state is on the move like lemmings towards the appliance room.

It was as we started arriving in the engine room that it became apparent that something very strange had happened. For a start, the young watchroom attendant was standing in the middle of the appliance room shaking with fear. But it was what he was standing in that drew all of our attention. He was literally standing in a huge pool of blood. In fact, as we were slowly waking up from our automatic mode we were noticing all sorts of strange things. There was blood splashed over the walls. Some of us had walked through it and a couple even had it smeared over themselves as a result of sliding down the pole, for it was even dripping down from the pole hole. It was everywhere. The place looked and smelt like a slaughter house.

In addition, there must have been about half a ton of horse manure spread about the place. It was on the fire appliances, on our uniforms, and mingled with the blood. In short it looked like a scene from hell. By this time the bells had stopped their clamour and we focused our attention on the watchroom attendant. He was still standing there as if he had had a visitation from the devil himself. The Guvnor, who had also arrived in the appliance room by this time, shouted at him to explain what the bloody hell was going on but he just stood there looking shocked. As our senses fully returned we assumed that this was just a wheeze that Dizzy had conjured up but, as he himself pointed out, he had responded to the bells just like the rest of us. Indeed, I remember him coming out of his room at the same time that several of us came out of the locker room.

Of course, still not convinced in the slightest that this was not down to the Guvnor, we started on the watchroom attendant. His story was very strange. He remembered being woken by a soft fluttering sound (a bleeding horse snuffling, I suppose!) He then said that he heard clip clopping in the station yard. (Guess what that is supposed to be?) Being the brave lad that he was, he decided not to investigate but to stay shut up in the watchroom. Eventually the clip clopping was sounding right outside the door, I suppose the horse was getting pissed off waiting for him to come out and so he was forced to get up and investigate. Didn`t want to be a complete wimp, did he? It was at that exact moment that the automatic call bells and lights activated. Now the alarm can only be sounded automatically from Headquarters or from within the watchroom itself. When the lights came on, he found himself standing in blood with some of it smeared on his body. Why he didn`t drop dead from fright we will never know. He was only a kid and as green as grass. The mystery remained as to how all of this happened, since the old man had been in his own room and the alarm sounded from the Headquarters' control. What we did know, as realisation dawned, was that phantom horses leave a lot of blood and shit lying around and it was going to have to be cleared up. Of course it fell to us and we had to work like slaves to have the station in its usual pristine condition ready for the oncoming watch.

The mystery was never solved. Dizzy swore that he had nothing to do with it and we have to admit it would have been difficult for him to have arranged it without someone knowing. It is impossible for firemen to keep a secret but this one was never solved. Some years later Dizzy emigrated to Australia and before he went he was asked by one of the lads about that night. "Honest to God I had nothing to do with it" he said. The fact he was taking the Lord's name in vain didn`t seem to bother him at all. Come to that it never bothered us either! Of course there are no such things as ghosts and particularly ghostly horse droppings and gallons of blood but some bugger knows who did it. I wouldn`t mind betting that this tale has been told a few times in bars 'down under' and by the one responsible for it too! Anyway whoever did it must have worked extremely hard at setting it up. Then again perhaps there were phantom horses that night!

AMSTERDAM (1)

There is only one reason why men go to Amsterdam, well two if you include football. Once again sitting around the mess table on a long boring night shift the conversations ranged over every subject known to man.

I was a Leading Fireman recently promoted and posted to Paddington Fire Station. It was the busiest Fire Station in the London Fire Brigade, although various other stations would no doubt dispute that. However, at this particular time it was the busiest and that was official. It was rare that the whole watch were in the station at the same time with four Fire Appliances, each of which was constantly being dispatched all over the west end of London and beyond. It was indeed rare to see other crews for more than an hour or so during a shift.

From time to time and for no reason whatsoever the calls would stop coming in and so, because this was one of those times, we found ourselves once again sitting at the mess table pontificating on every subject in the world. Mick, one of our more worldly wise Firemen, was reminiscing of his time spent in Amsterdam. He had travelled all over the world in his capacity as a Pipe band drum major as well as national Service in the Army and his stories were always worth listening to.

His tales of Amsterdam were of the most interest of course with stories about jazz clubs, drinking and of course women! He whetted our appetite so thoroughly it was decided there and then that the Firemen of Amsterdam would be contacted and some sort of 'cultural' visit arranged.

It took several weeks to set up, but finally it was arranged and we were to take a Fire Engine to Amsterdam and give a display of our skills. Part of the display was the use of hook ladders which the Dutch firemen had never seen. These ladders were used to scale a building from the outside and there was no limit on the height, other than the height of the building itself, to which they could be used. The visit also entailed a football match and a visit to a museum. The highlight of course would then be to sample the nightlife of the red light district of Amsterdam.

The journey to Amsterdam more or less set the tone of the trip. As well as the Fire Appliance carrying a crew of six there was also a personnel carrier with another dozen or so who were not going to be left behind, the allure of the red light district being too much! Before we reached Harwich, where we were to catch the ferry to the Hook of Holland, most of the men were as pissed as parrots, and we hadn't got to the duty free stuff yet!

Once on the boat we more or less took over one of the bars and drank our way steadily across the North Sea. Arriving at the Hook of Holland it will probably come as no surprise when I say that two of our members were unconscious and had to be carried off the ferry. They were unceremoniously dumped on to a luggage cart and towed to customs where the customs officers somewhat graciously passed us through without any problems because we were 'respectable' Firemen.

Having passed through customs, and of course this was before the days of the E.U. and its open borders, just in case you are wondering what the hell I'm talking about, we drove to Amsterdam and arrived at the big Fire Station in the centre of the city called 'Y tunnel 4'. There we were welcomed by several Dutch Firemen and shown where we could put our gear. Dutch Fireman have their own rooms, at least on this fire station they did, and several had kindly doubled up elsewhere so that we had rooms to sleep in. We were only going to be there for two nights so we more or less started the program straight away.

After a drink, coffee and tea that is, we gave our display. The Guvnor and I made up the hook ladder crew and we climbed up to the top of their six floor training tower. As they had never seen hook ladders they were most impressed and were equally impressed when the whole crew carried out a simulated fire drill in their station yard using the London Fire Appliance. Once all the drilling was out of the way it was time for dinner. The Dutch fireman had prepared an excellent meal for us.

During the meal a couple of Dutchmen thought they would have some fun at our expense and started flicking peas at us. What they had no way of knowing was that throwing food around is almost obligatory on a London Station and within seconds they were wearing soup, potatoes and anything else within reach. It took the intervention of a couple of the more serious minded to stop it escalating into a punch-up. So much for a friendly cultural exchange.

As the evening was still relatively young it was decided to play a game of football in their magnificent gym. Having lost the food fight they were now intent on winning the game and I have to say that in the technical sense they played very well, showing skills and control few of us could match. What they lacked though were the basic hooligan skills which we had in abundance; after all, didn't the British invent football hooliganism? In fact, we kicked their sorry arses all over the gym; so much for skill! I even scored the winning goal.

The day drew to a close and we were pleased to eventually get our heads down. The accumulating effect of too much alcohol, little sleep and travelling for about fifteen hours was taking its toll; not to mention a game of football. The next day was the day we were really in Amsterdam for and it certainly turned into one that has remained indelibly printed on my brain!

What had been arranged for us was a visit to the famous Amsterdam Museum and in the evening, after spending the day doing some sightseeing around the red light district, we were going to be taken to a night club. The day ended for me with a black eye, nearly being shot and finally being sprayed with a chemical protection spray that nearly asphyxiated me! First let me describe the visit to the museum and a most embarrassing moment for the London Fire Brigade!

We were given a guided tour of the museum by the director himself. Not being too culturally minded the majority of us were glad when it came to an end and we all trouped off to a large reception area for refreshments. There were paintings and works of art all over the place worth millions and the director took great pleasure in detailing some of the more famous pieces. Tea and coffee was served to us using a solid silver antique set which was probably priceless. The conversation flowed and more tea and coffee was served. At this point someone wanted more sugar but the sugar container, which was a beautiful solid silver dish complete with lid and engraved with the coat of arms of one of the families who used to control Amsterdam, had disappeared!

There were several museum personnel in the room as well as a number of Dutch Firemen and with the London contingent there must have been 20 people there and we all started looking for the bloody thing. After a minute or so of searching there followed an embarrassing silence when it dawned on everyone present that it must have been nicked!

No one said anything but everyone was looking at everyone else and it became decidedly uncomfortable. There then came some movement at the end of the room and one of our men, I'll call him 'Freshy', realising the game was up; put his hand in his overcoat pocket and came out with the sugar jar. Without seemingly being the least concerned he simply walked to the table and placed it on the tray, picked up a cup of coffee and acted as if nicking a priceless piece of silver was an everyday occurrence! No one said anything and the silence was eventually broken when the director decided that the visit had come to an end and we were escorted out. We were never invited back!

We went back to the Fire Station to wash and change and then on to a bar prior to going to the night club. The grog flowed freely and I was, without a doubt, more than a little sloshed and having imbibed copious amounts of lager it was time for a pee, and so off I wandered down the bar looking for the toilet. Now I don't remember upsetting anyone on the way to the toilet but someone must have taken a dislike to me for some reason for just as I had finished doing what I had gone in there for I heard a noise behind me and turned my head just in time to receive a cracking blow to my face that knocked me cold. I came to a minute or two later to find one of my pals kneeling over me. Because I had taken so long he had become worried and found me lying on the toilet floor senseless!

He helped me stagger back out into the bar passing a table where four men were sitting. The looks and smirks left me in little doubt who had been responsible for my now furiously aching head and swelling eye. Looking around the bar I found that the rest of my loyal friends had buggered off to the night club chaperoned by the Dutch firemen. They had assumed that we knew where the club was but no one had checked and so my mate and I were cast adrift in Amsterdam more than three parts drunk and not having a clue where we were.

We had a few more drinks and decided that the best course of action was to get back to the Fire Station and obtain directions to the nightclub. Our problem was that we didn't know where the fire station was! I had the address, Y tunnel 4, but the pronunciation in Dutch was most definitely different in cockney and as a result we just couldn't make ourselves understood.

We were wandering all over Amsterdam, more drunk than sober, soaking wet and freezing cold. Did I mention that it was always pouring down with rain in Holland? It seems to me that Holland must be the wettest bloody place in the world! I have been in the country many times and it has always been pissing down! In addition, my head was throbbing like mad both from too much drink and the good hiding I had taken in the pub.

I was fading fast and Den, my mate, pulled me into a doorway to get out of the pouring rain and try to work out just where we were. We had been standing there for a minute or so when the door opened and a rather attractive woman asked what we were doing. I just couldn't be bothered to reply. I was too busy dying! But Den gave her the whole story including the bit about being lost.

She suggested that we go inside and get dry and maybe have a drink! Now I may have been half drunk and not quite with it, but I didn't need a degree in human relations to twig what was going on. Den was all for it and dragged me in. I have to admit that I didn't need much 'dragging' but not for the reason most readers of this tale would think! I was in fact in a very sorry state, freezing, soaking wet and really just about semi-conscious. The thought of somewhere warm and dry was just too much and so I allowed myself to be pulled in.

Once inside, the women who had invited us in led me to the first floor and suggested I take off my clothes! I told her that I wasn't interested in sex or anything else and she turned decidedly nasty. She demanded money for me being there and became most agitated when I told her to "fuck off!" Not particularly gentlemanly I must admit but the reader must take into consideration my delicate state and her very aggressive attitude. I just wanted to be warm and dry.

The whole situation deteriorated dramatically when she suddenly stuck a gun in my face and demanded that I give her money. It says a lot for my state of mind and how I felt that I again simply said "fuck off!" Had I been anywhere near sane and sober I would almost certainly have fainted with fright! It was at this point the other woman suddenly appeared and probably saved me from getting my head shot off. What happened next though left me feeling that a bullet between the eyes would have been more preferable. Without a word, she held up a can of what I assume was a pepper spray or something similar. The effect was immediate and totally disabling. I was blinded, couldn't breathe and my face felt like it was burning.

I vaguely remember falling down the stairs and stumbling out into the rain where I lay in the gutter desperately splashing water into my eyes and on my face. It was there that my mate found me a few minutes later. He helped me to stand and we staggered off down the road like two drunken idiots, not far from the truth as it happens.

How we found our way back to the fire station, I have no recollection. I was wet, freezing cold and suffering from several injuries. Any sane person would have sought out a hospital but I settled for the back of a transit van in the fire station yard and collapsed semi-conscious on the floor.

When I awoke with the worst headache I had ever had in my life Dennis was already sitting up and contemplating his private parts. I looked and couldn't quite comprehend what it was I was looking at. It turned out to be a rather wrinkled and grubby looking condom firmly attached to his penis! It turned out that this really was what all the trouble had been about.

When we had gone into the flat with the women, the girl he was with had, apparently, immediately asked him to put on the condom. Being fairly drunk he must have done so but had no recollection, until now, of doing it. She then invited him to bed but at that point he realised what was happening and declined. The girl then started to get angry and Dennis, in no uncertain terms, told her that he wasn't interested. It was at this point the girl apparently heard me telling the girl upstairs to 'fuck off'. Presumably I had said it rather loudly and she rushed up with the gas canister. The rest, as they say, is history.

Believe me the whole story is true, how could you make up a story like that? When we met up with the rest of the men they told us that they had had a great time in the night club and why hadn't we gone along. When we told our tale there was a lot of leg pulling and laughing. It turned out that they had had a great time in a club, free food, drink and at least three floor shows.   Den and I on the other hand had nearly been murdered, but that I suppose was the luck of the draw.

AMSTERDAM (2)

Following the disaster of my first trip to Amsterdam and having to listen to the great time everyone else had out there, I resolved to organise another trip and this time try and get there and back in one piece. Mick and I were the motivators once again and most of those who had been on the first trip also wanted a second helping.

Once again the Dutch Firemen were contacted and a date for a visit was arranged. Because of what had happened to me on the first trip I had gained a level of fame or perhaps I should say notoriety! My adventures had made me a bit of a celebrity and in any event, I was always at the forefront of anything which was going on.

I made sure that on this trip I remained at least partly sober and should anyone have even looked at me oddly I was going to get in the first punch! Fortunately it never came to that and after more or less the same routine as on the first trip we found ourselves at a night club. It was obvious that Dutch Firemen have some influence regarding permits to operate etc. and owners of nightclubs obviously found it to be to their benefit to curry favour with the Firemen. As a result of this' favouritism' about twenty of us trouped into this rather upmarket club in the middle of the red light district without having to pay, simply as guests of the Dutch Firemen.

The club itself was organised on four levels. The ground floor was for drinking and food and for playing, of all things, Bingo! The slight difference was that there seemed to be an awful lot of near naked women wandering about helping men fill out their cards! I kid you not but we played bingo there and you had to fill a card completely to win a fairly substantial amount of money. We were all given free cards but not one of us got near winning, unfortunately. It was whilst we were in this section that one of the Dutch

Firemen decided he wanted to have a stand-up fight with me, all very friendly and a sort of competitive pastime this particular Fireman excelled at. I seem to attract these nutters wherever I go! The idea was that I could have the first punch and if he were still to be standing it would be his turn. Quite honestly the thought of playing this particular game frightened the bloody life out of me. He was built like a Dutch barn and his face bore the marks of what must have been a lifetime of bare knuckle fist fights!

I didn't want to back down in front of everyone but at the same time didn't want to end up in the local emergency unit. I suggested to him that he have the first punch and he readily agreed. I thought that as obviously me hitting him was going to have no effect whatsoever, I could use the excuse of being near comatose after he had hit me for not putting up a good show. I must have been quite pissed even to have thought like that! It was to my everlasting relief that a couple of other Dutch Firemen, knowing how deadly this man was, persuaded him that killing an English Fireman in a public place probably wasn't a good idea! I was beginning to think that Amsterdam wasn't really my cup of tea!

Having got out of having my features permanently altered by Rocky Marciano the whole lot of us trouped up to the next level where they were showing blue films. There was another bar in this section and we merrily drank up whilst watching a selection of Amsterdam's artwork. I was still a little edgy at my earlier encounter and wondered what was going to happen next. Fortunately nothing did and after about an hour of films we moved on to the next level which was a straightforward porn display between a man and women.

Having had several drinks and having escaped having my head bashed in my courage was returning and I started with the smart assed jokes and comments directed at the performers on stage. Surprisingly they took it all in good part and I even got some sort of repartee going between the actor and myself. The woman was a bit frosty but it didn't put him off his stroke all! In general it was all good fun and we were then invited up to the top floor for another show. On the way I was stopped by a couple of Dutch Firemen and they wanted to know how I was enjoying it etc. Immediately suspicious I said it was great, quite an experience and that there wasn't anything in the U.K. to match it, legally anyway. I was also alert to the fact that I was about to be beaten up for some reason or other but this time it was all very friendly. I was becoming paranoid! Another couple of minutes chatting and we drifted up to the next show. As I entered the theatre it was now obvious why I had been held up. Every seat was taken except for one at the front, nearest the stage. I had no choice but to take it and wondered why it had been left for me. I had an idea and sure enough it was confirmed when a woman came on to the stage and dancing to music stripped off. I caught her eye looking at someone behind me and then her eyes flicked to me and I knew I was the one being set up.

First of all she invited another woman up on to the stage who supposedly was a member of the public but only an idiot would have believed she was. In short order she also was stripped off and they started pawing and exploring each other in a somewhat personal manner! The whole time this was going on I was wondering how I fitted in to the scheme of things. I didn't have to wait long.

After a few minutes they both came down off the stage and whilst pretending to be randomly molesting men in the audience they were obviously converging on me. Sure enough one of them sat on my lap and the other was rubbing her hands over my body, much to the amusement of everyone there. Then they started to pull me towards the stage. The obvious intention was to embarrass me as much as possible before I cracked and backed away in embarrassment. What they didn't know was that I was crazier than they were. As we got to the stage I held them both off and made them stand still whilst to the music I slowly did a striptease in front of a couple of hundred people.

Amidst much catcalling and filthy remarks I did as suggestive a performance as is possible for a six footer Fireman who didn't care a shit. The two girls didn't know what to do and eventually joined in the applause. It was also the signal for several others of my mates to join in. Without further ado they were up on the stage stripping off and grabbing women all over the place. Someone produced several bottles of baby oil and the place became like a bleeding Roman orgy!!! I hasten to add that I could see this coming and had grabbed my clothes and got off the stage quick. I got behind the bar and watched the antics unfold. I knew I had made the right decision when at the end of all these frolics a couple of my mates were without trousers. Someone had pinched them!

The night more or less ended there and we made our way back to the fire station for a couple of hours sleep before the trip back to the U.K. The lads who had lost trousers were supplied with some uniform Dutch trousers by a couple of Dutch firemen who took pity on them. This second trip to Amsterdam was of course a much pleasanter trip than my first, but each in its own way has left me with memories I shall never forget.

WHERE IS MICK?

This story involves a particular Fireman who, as nature decrees, is so good looking he has only to look at a woman and immediately she falls in love with him! He never had to do anything, just stand there and women would swoon. Tall and dark with those drooping 'come to bed eyes'. Everyone on the station envied the ease with which women were attracted to him. He didn't have the 'gift of the gab', he didn't need it.

This particular nightshift saw him driving one of the appliances with me and another Fireman sitting in the back and the Guvnor up front. Around midnight, sure enough, down went the bells and off we went, bells ringing and sirens wailing, to an address just off Bayswater. We had been called to a fire in one of the many bedsits that abound in the area and because of the fire risk of the area several other appliances were also ordered to the address.

As it turned out there was no fire, or at least, nothing too serious. It was a smouldering cable in an electrical junction box and one that didn't need the administrations of half the London Fire Brigade! All the other appliances were sent back to their stations but we remained to check out the junction box and surrounding rooms and staircases, just in case!

From out of a room which joined the staircase a rather fetching young woman came to enquire if all was well and if she could make us a coffee or something! I thought that there was a slight emphasis on the 'something' but put it down to my over active imagination. 'Mick' was all for a coffee, but the Guvnor knowing the sort of problems that could develop, gracefully declined on our behalf and so we went about our inspections and searches. We were told to complete our work and, once satisfied all was safe and no further risk of a fire, meet back at the appliance.

About half an hour later me and the other Fireman as well as the Guvnor were back but, yes that's right, no 'Mick'. "Where the bloody hell is he?" the 'boss' asked though like us he probably guessed!

Another ten minutes passed and the boss, whose patience was running very thin, ordered the other fireman to go and find him. No sooner had this fireman disappeared than Mick turned up. Right, said the boss I can bloody guess what you have been up to so you might as well give all the details!

"Well, said 'Mick' "you'll never believe it and it's a first for me, that girl who invited us in for a coffee, well after you lot had buggered off she came out again and of course we started chatting and she invited me in, just to have a look around. What could I do? Well, one thing led to another. We were on the couch and she gave me the best blow job I've ever had in my life! Honestly I have never had one like it before. After I calmed down we cuddled a bit and my hands started wandering, you know, up her skirt and generally groping around. Well, was I surprised when I found the biggest pair of bollocks you can imagine! I could barely take it in! This pretty young woman was a fucking man and had just given me a great blow job! I didn't know whether to smack him in the face or tell him how nice it had been! I decided neither and with as much composure as I could I left and made my way back here". We all thought the story hilarious and only 'Mick' could have managed it. His attraction, it seemed, went beyond women and extended to transsexuals too!

A rather humorous postscript was to follow. The Fireman sent to find 'Mick' returned a short while later and couldn't help but start boasting about the girl who had offered us coffee. He said that she had met him on the stairs, and like 'Mick' she had invited him in to have a look around. He said, with almost wonder in his voice, how she touched him, arousing him and giving him deep, wet throat massaging kisses. He said he had never felt so horny in his life!

Perhaps the reader can imagine how this young Fireman reacted when told about 'Mick's' exploits and the 'fabulous blow job' just a few minutes before his 'deep throat experience'! He looked as if he wanted to throw up but held on until we returned to the station, but once back he was off like a rocket to the shower room where we think he probably scrubbed his mouth and throat all the way down to his rectum with carbolic soap!!

FIREMEN FROM MARS

Believe it or not the breathing apparatus used by Firemen, at least in the London Fire Brigade, was, with one or two modifications the same piece of equipment used by our forebears a hundred years earlier. I had better quickly add that they have all now been replaced by modern air sets.

The breathing apparatus set was an oxygen re-breather and without getting too technical it meant that a small cylinder of oxygen could, in practice, last for many hours in an emergency situation. In normal circumstances it would last for up to an hour. The Firemen used and trusted this set as it really was very reliable. There were one or two drawbacks such as not being able to see, talk, smell or hear and the bloody thing weighed about forty pounds and was as uncomfortable as hell to wear, other than that it was great!

The wearer couldn't see because the goggles were virtually opaque! This rather stupid situation was brought about because just about every day the goggles would be checked and cleaned and often given a coating of anti-mist cream. Rubbing this cream onto the lens with a dirty finger was a little like rubbing an optical lens with a piece of sandpaper!

The wearer couldn't talk because once the set was being worn it meant that the mouthpiece, which was exactly the same as that on a Frogman's diving apparatus was firmly fixed into the mouth and held by the teeth. This always resulted in copious amounts of dribble and an aching jaw. How we managed to communicate as a crew is still a source of absolute wonder to me, but somehow we did.

As for smell, well I suppose it was necessary to wear a quite powerfully sprung nose clip to stop smoke being inhaled through the nose, not much point in having a sealed mouth if the smoke can get in another way. The problem with this was that as well as all the dribble from the mouthpiece there was always a huge build-up of mucous because of the pressure of the nose clip and when the bloody thing was removed the torrent of stuff that exited from the nose was incredible! It also left two lovely bright red marks on the nostrils which remained there for days.

As for hearing, well by definition the apparatus was worn in dense smoke and the effect of dense smoke on noise is to deaden it appreciably. The weight was just another cross to bear. One last point: when the set was being worn it made a loud 'clicking' noise. This noise came from two valves which allowed the oxygen to pass into the lungs and also 'clicked' on the exhale to stop the exhaled breath going back the way it had come, a simple arrangement but noisy. There we have it, deaf, dumb, dribbly, making a funny clicking noise and looking like the creature from the black lagoon!!! In this thing we had to search for people who might be trapped in fires and smoke-logged buildings.

We were called to a fire just around the back of Paddington railway station. When we arrived, it was obvious from the smoke pouring from several windows that there was a serious fire somewhere in the building and of course it was our job to go in, find it and put it out. Alongside this part of our work it was also essential that crews started searching for people who may be trapped. As the building was one of those cheap hotels which abound in the Paddington area there was a strong possibility that there would be someone in one of the many rooms and it was our job to find and of course rescue them.

I, along with two other Firemen, was detailed to put on breathing apparatus and start searching. We worked and remained together as a crew the whole time and there were several other breathing apparatus crews detailed as well to search other parts of the building. While we would be stumbling about in the pitch black, blind, deaf and dumb, kicking down doors, searching for people trapped, the firefighting crews would be tackling the fire. We started our search on the ground floor which was heavily smoke logged and spent a good deal of time searching each room carefully. People do the strangest of things in fires and will hide under beds and even climb into wardrobes and cupboards in their search for safety. Each room would take several minutes to check out and of course, because of the drawbacks to the breathing sets I have described, these searches were done completely by touch. We couldn't see and, other than the loud clicking of the sets, couldn't hear much at all. In this blind stumbling fashion, somehow, each room would be thoroughly searched.

Having searched the ground floor we carried on to a staircase which led to the basement and yet more rooms. We made our way down the stairs hanging on to each other in the knowledge that if we lost contact with each other it was possible to become completely disorientated, eventually run out of oxygen and slowly suffocate, not a prospect to dwell on. So, like the proverbial three blind mice we hung on to each other like men possessed! We made our way down the stairs 'clicking' and breathing hard like marathon runners, funny how fear makes you breathe hard!

We had been in the basement for about 15 minutes and had searched several rooms when we came to yet another room which was locked. It was fairly standard procedure with a locked room to knock very loudly on the door in the vain hope it would be quickly opened. In practice the loud knock would be usually followed several seconds later by a fireman delivering a strong kick and smashing it open. And so it was with this particular door.

The leader of the crew, holding on to me and the other fireman for balance and leverage, with one mighty kick knocked the door almost completely off its hinges. What happened next has gone down in folk lore and makes me laugh every time I think of it. There was a very loud scream, obviously a woman's scream and the decibel level must have shattered half the windows in Paddington. This was followed by a man's voice on the edge of hysteria and definitely in a foreign accent.

I was the last man in the crew and realising that whatever the problem was, it wasn't smoke! I lifted my useless goggles just in time to see a well-built man, completely naked, launch himself across the room and proceed to rain karate chops and kicks on my crew members. The woman in the meantime, also naked and lying on the bed, was still screaming her bloody head off!! There wasn't a wisp of smoke in the room and with the lights on it was as clear as the proverbial bell!

My two crew members were being slowly beaten up by this lunatic who had attacked them and the only reason they were, up to this point, not seriously injured was that they were somewhat protected by the breathing apparatus set and their fire helmets. I was the only one of the three of us who realised what was happening; my two mates were as confused as could possibly be and had no comprehension at all as to what was going on other than being pummelled rather violently.

As quickly as I could I removed my mouthpiece and, dribble permitting, did my best to try and calm the situation. My voice had some sort of calming effect because the man attacking my partners stopped his attack, stood there with a glazed look in his eyes then backed off a little. The daft cow on the bed continued to scream until the man returned to the bed to calm her.

Eventually my two mates were also able to remove their goggles and mouthpieces and take in the situation. There we were, three rather grubby firemen in a well-lit and smoke free bedroom with mucous and dribble running down our faces and a naked couple sitting on the bed staring at us. There was an obvious need for us to explain why we had burst into their room and this we did as quickly and calmly as possible. The last thing we now wanted was for them to think they were going to be burnt to death in a fire!!

I asked the man why he had attacked us? You never know, a piece of information like that could be useful in the future! He said that his wife had been asleep and he was reading when suddenly the door crashed open and in barged, what he could only describe, as three monsters from Mars!! Dressed completely in black with huge opaque staring eyes with tubes running from their faces and making a loud 'clicking' noise, just what was he supposed to have thought? He had never seen a London fireman so had no idea what one looked like and in any event having no knowledge of a fire in the hotel why would he think firemen would kick his door down anyway? Reasonable I suppose! He said that it was purely reaction why he had attacked us and that he had been terrified by these figures storming into their room.

His wife by now had calmed but was obviously still very upset and it took a lot of talking to convince them both that the safest place was to stay right there and that we would stay with them until it was safe to leave. We did stay and eventually we even got them to laugh about what had happened and no doubt when they returned to whichever country they had come from had quite a story to tell.

TAKEN FOR A RIDE

The stories in this book are all about what I consider to be funny events in the London Fire Brigade. This particular story is about me getting to work so although extremely tenuous there is a Fire Brigade connection.

To get to work I used to ride my pedal bike to the local railway station and put the bike in the baggage car. That way, when I arrived at Charing Cross, I could get across the middle of London to my station relatively easily.

This particular day I arrived at Tonbridge station and as usual the London train was waiting. I looked for the Guard to obtain his permission to put my bike in the baggage van. It always seemed the right thing to do. I'm not sure that I actually needed his permission but it was always 'politick' and in any event polite to do so. As it turned out he was nowhere to be found so I put my bike in the baggage van and went and found a seat. Not finding the Guard wasn't unusual and had happened many times before so I thought no more about it.

There were still about ten minutes to go before the train left for London and more passengers were still boarding. It was about then that the Guard put in an appearance. He entered the carriage and started checking tickets and when he got to me demanded to know, quite aggressively, if it was my bike in the baggage van, bit silly really given that I was sitting there dressed up in bike gear and a crash helmet on my lap! Having no reason to deny it and dressed as I was it would also have been stupid not to admit it. It was patently obvious that he considered himself to be very important and also a vital cog in the smooth running of British Rail. I bet most commuters have met this sort of person at one time or another.

I realised that antagonising this epitome of Railway efficiency wouldn't be the right thing to do so for once I held on to my temper and simply replied that, yes, it was my bike. Not content with my reply he wanted to know who gave me permission to load a bike on to his train. I explained that as he wasn't around, gaining permission was impossible so I did the only thing I could do, which was to put the bike in the van. I could almost hear his brain grinding away in search of any other transgression or violation of Railway procedures and his eyes lit up when he thought he had reason to put me in irons or at least lecture me further. "Has it got a label on it then?" was the next gem he came out with. I simply replied that there was a label. (In all the years I travelled with my bike I never found out why I had to put a label on it with my name and address (I knew who I was and where I lived). I wanted to add some sarcastic remark but decided, for once, to hold my tongue.

Obviously quite peeved that I had complied with BR regulations but still not happy that I had put the bike in the van without his explicit permission he just simply said that I had to get off the train and take my bike with me. "Why?" I reasonably asked. I must say again at this point that I hadn't raised my voice or argued in any way. "Because you put it there without my permission", he bellowed. I explained again that as he was nowhere to be found, I did the only thing I could do under the circumstances and put my bike in the van. I also added that in any event I wasn't going to get off the train, no matter what he said.

He was now truly agitated with my refusal to get off and the next thought that entered his head was to ask for my ticket, which I showed him. He tried to take the ticket from me but I decided that showing him the ticket was all he was entitled to and in any event, I didn't trust him to give it back! Thwarted he yet again ordered me off the train and, when I once more refused, took a step towards me and said "I can throw you off if you refuse". Now he was talking my language! I quietly told him that should he touch me in any way it would result in something he most definitely would not like. Maybe it was the quiet way I said it or maybe the look on my face but he took a quick step backwards and obviously the thought of violence slipped quickly from his mind. Shame, I thought!

The train was now about due to leave but the Guard was only interested in getting me off, no matter what, and when I again refused, told me that not only was the train not leaving because of my refusal to get off, but he was going to inform all the passengers that the train was cancelled and that they were to get off and wait for another train to London and that the responsibility for this was mine. This man was obviously half crazy and I wondered at the recruitment process of British Rail.

I really didn't care what he did for by now I had resolved that nothing was going to get me off this train and I would sit there all night if necessary. He duly made the announcement over the speaker system and the train emptied, apart from me of course. Having asserted his authority in emptying the train he came back to me and blamed me for inconveniencing all those who had got off and he was now going to call the Police. Again I resisted losing my temper and just told him to do whatever he wished, I was staying put!

About five minutes later back he came with a Policeman. "This is him" he said and, given that I was the only one on the train, I thought the Policeman showed great restraint in not making a sarcastic remark of his own! "Good evening sir, I understand there is a problem" he said. Absolutely deadpan and perfect, a copper with his head screwed on I thought. I went through the whole story and added the 'clincher' that I thought the Guard had been drinking and that was why he was so belligerent. As I said, a copper with his head screwed on the right way. He asked to see my ticket, just as a matter of form really and told the incredulous Guard that he didn't think I had committed any offence and it was a railway affair. With that he left.

The guard was still standing there wondering what to do next when a railway official arrived, the Station Manager I think, and demanded to know what the hell was going on and why hadn't the train left ten minutes ago. The Guard ran through the story yet again or at least his version of it. The Station manager went through the routine of asking to see my ticket as well as asking for my version of events and for good measure I included the bit about the Policeman and that I thought the Guard was inebriated.

The Station Manager reflected on this for a moment and realised that in all probability the Guard had been drinking and also that he was being unreasonable. In no uncertain terms he told the Guard that he wanted "this fucking train moving in the next minute or there would be real trouble". He stormed off the train no doubt to rearrange timetables that had undoubtedly been disrupted by the hold up.

The Guard now suitably cowed and possibly fearing for his job, left and contacted the driver. I felt the train tremble as the power engaged and the train started to move. Within seconds we were speeding alongside the platform on our way to London. I say we and by that I mean the Guard, me and of course the driver. As we sped down the platform I couldn't help but chuckle at the looks on all the stunned faces of the passengers still standing on the platform whom the guard had told to disembark. It was unfortunate for them of course and no doubt caused an awful lot of inconvenience but it amused me tremendously. Such things only happen in films, well usually! I had my own personal train the whole way to London and the Guard didn't trouble me any further. I did expect to find my bike in bits when we arrived but I suppose the guard thought better of it.

I had several run-ins with, usually, half-drunk guards on British rail over the years but that incident was by far the funniest. I think it fair to say that there were also very considerate and reasonable guards on British rail, though I rarely met them!

DIDN'T SEE ANYTHING OFFICER

It wasn't often I found myself disliking another Fireman. Over the years there were many that I wouldn't have chosen to be best pals with but actively disliking someone was rare. Unfortunately there was one that I just kept coming across who simply pissed me off every time I met him. It seemed to be some sort of magical happening that we kept meeting up. I won't name him because as much as I disliked him I wouldn't want to embarrass him, though he was a prat. Should he ever read this book though I'm sure he will recognise himself as the detested one. In fact I have never met anyone who liked him. He would be discussed and always the consensus was that he is a prat of the first order. The strange thing was that he would help anyone and had a jovial and happy nature and was always trying to be someone's best friend, maybe that was the trouble. Sad, isn't it?

I first met him when we were both Firemen at Kensington and whilst he was tolerated on the watch everyone would have preferred him to have been on another watch. He was just that sort of person. I was eventually promoted to leading Fireman and posted to Paddington but who should turn up a few months later on a transfer? I couldn't believe it. In fact he seemed to plague me wherever I went in the Brigade. He turned up at Euston, at the training centre and I even came across him countless times by accident at fires or on courses. Everywhere I went he was there or subsequently turned up, I couldn't get rid of the bastard. I suppose it was written that this man was destined to nearly kill me!

As part of my career development I was offered a place at the Fire Service College, Morton-in-Marsh. I say offered because had I not gone I would have been ordered to go at some time in the future when it probably wouldn't have suited me, so I accepted. Who should be in the same training syndicate when I arrived? Right again! I was going to have to put up with him for the next six weeks!

As soon as he saw me it was 'best friend time'. He was like a puppy dog with two tails finding me there amongst all the other guys from Brigades all over the country, none of whom he knew of course. He latched on to me like a leech and as I have already said I didn't want to hurt his feelings so simply went along with it with some degree of bonhomie, difficult though it was.

I had gone up to Morton by train and he had gone up by car. Getting to the College wasn't the simplest thing on the planet and when 'ole pain in the arse' offered to drive me back to London every weekend as well as collect me for the return journey I jumped at the chance. I said I didn't like him but I'm not stupid, so turning down a free lift every weekend whilst at the same time claiming my travel expenses didn't bother my conscience at all. I always made sure I had a book for the journey so this way I could ignore him as much as possible because he did tend to prattle on in the most boring fashion. In fact he was always babbling on! The reader may well think I am being totally ungracious about this man but I can assure you that the average person would have committed suicide bottled up in a car with this man for anything over ten minutes and I had to endure it for about three hours, but I'm made of sterner stuff and anyway I was thinking of all my free travel expenses.

It was on the final return trip to London that he nearly killed me. As I have said, repeatedly, the man was a bloody fool. We had completed the course and were now driving back towards London. I, as usual, had my head in a book but became aware that we were flying along far in excess of any legal speed limit. As there was only a seat belt and a windscreen between me and eternity, I thought I had better start taking an interest in what is going on. It was obvious that he had entered into some sort of race with a black guy driving a Ford transit.

I was alternately being thrust back into my seat then thrown against the tension of the seatbelt by this bloody drag race we had embarked on. The transit would scream past and cut in front of our car, and with a shout of 'bastard' sometimes proceeded by 'black', although the reader must understand that this wasn't a racist comment rather a term of abstract recognition! We both have friends of all shades so shouting out 'black bastard' didn't hold any real significance at all!

This race had been going on for several minutes and I was absolutely convinced it was going to end in disaster. My driver was becoming ever more excited and the risks he was taking were making my hair stand on end. It had become something like some video game and sure enough was going to end like one.

I was still trying to remain calm and relaxed whilst at the same time preparing to meet my maker. The end came suddenly and all too predictably. I saw it coming, it was so bloody obvious, but before I could utter a word it was too late. We approached a roundabout at just below the speed of sound and about six feet behind the transit. There wasn't any other traffic on the roundabout and so the stage was set for the final act.

I saw the brake lights flick on in front of me as the transit braked on entering the roundabout, my chauffeur immediately braked hard to avoid running in to him but at that moment the transits brake lights went off and the van accelerated hard away. Dopey ceased braking immediately and accelerated hard after the van in an attempt to catch and overtake and it was at that precise point as dopey was accelerating that the transit braked hard and screeched to a halt.

As we were only several meters behind and still accelerating there wasn't a hope in hell of avoiding smashing into the van and we slammed into the back of it with a thunderous crash. The windscreen imploded into the passenger compartment and the engine block and bonnet were unceremoniously shoved back trapping my legs and right arm. At the same time my head struck the side post and I momentarily blacked out. I came to a minute or two later unable to move but registered that I wasn't feeling any pain so thought things could be worse!! My first sight of the world I was rejoining was 'stupid' standing looking at his wrecked car and bemoaning the fact it was now just a heap of junk. He was actually repeating over and over "my car, my car"! The fool wasn't in the least concerned about yours truly who was still trapped inside it.

People appeared from all over the place and several cars stopped amongst which were several other Firemen, themselves on their way back to London after also finishing at Morton-in-Marsh. Fortunately they took to the task of getting me out of the car like the true professionals they were and using tools, jacks and their bare hands had me out of the wreck and sitting against the crash barrier in no time. Dopey was by now almost in tears over the state of his car and I wasn't feeling any compassion for him in the slightest given how gullible he had been in trying to give the transit driver a hard time and not least of all because he still hadn't enquired as to my wellbeing. That was probably just as well, as given the black mood I was in, it was better we were kept apart.

It was whilst I was sitting there that the black driver came over to me and said "I'm sorry man I had nothing personal against you but your mate just really pissed me off". "I just hope that he learns from this and don't mess with no fucking niggers again." This all came out in that lovely Caribbean twang and I couldn't help but smile and said that I didn't bear him any grudge either and on the other hand it was shame he hadn't killed the dipstick who had been driving me. I still was not feeling kindly disposed towards my driver!! With a smile he wandered off and was promptly grabbed by a couple of traffic coppers.

I sat and watched them talking to him and eventually one of the Policemen came over to me and said they were going to 'nail' this black bastard and would I make a statement that he had deliberately caused the accident by his driving and braking. There were two things I didn't like about this.

The first was that when he used the term 'black bastard' he didn't mean it as a term of endearment or casual comment. It was simply because he was black. Now I can hate a black, yellow, brown or white person with equal passion. It simply depends on the individual. Secondly the twat who was at least 50% to blame for the accident would have got off scot-free and my sense of fair play wouldn't allow that. Lastly I was still severely pissed off that I had nearly been killed and Dopey had still not enquired as to how I was.

I told the copper that as far as I was concerned the van had simply braked at the roundabout and we had slammed into the back of him because we were driving too fast. Anything else I hadn't noticed because I was reading my book. The copper couldn't believe it! In fact, he didn't believe it and again tried to get me to say that the black guy was at fault. I was having none of it though and insisted I hadn't seen anything until the windscreen had imploded.

By now there were fire engines and even an ambulance had turned up but all I was interested in was going home. Apart from some cuts, bruises and torn clothes I was in remarkably good shape and turned down offers of a trip to the local hospital. Instead I prevailed upon a couple of Firemen in one of the other cars to give me a lift the rest of the way back to London. I grabbed my kit from the wreck and piled in and off we went.

I never found out the outcome of the accident. Whether my driver was prosecuted or if indeed the black guy was. In truthfulness I didn't care a sod if they had both been prosecuted; they deserved to be. It was about a year or so later that I came across Dopey again when he turned up as an instructor at the Training centre. He never mentioned the accident and neither did I and so I concluded from that he didn't come out of it well. After all unless there are witnesses to the contrary the driver who runs into the back of another motorist is usually to blame!

One last thought: this bloody fool was now an instructor at the brigade's training school; time for me to retire me thinks!!

TRIP TO SPAIN

This story is loosely connected to my time in the Brigade in that I had just retired from it, so that is my excuse for including it as one of my Fire Brigade stories. Doesn't get much looser than that I suppose.

Never one to simply look a gift horse in the mouth I was prepared to jump down its throat when Pam, my wife, came home from work one day and said we had a chance of a free holiday in Spain. Pam was a lawyer and one of her long-standing clients had offered her the use of his villa in southern Spain. Pam had handled several divorces and various other problems for him and he was showing his appreciation by the offer. Pam, as usual, and as ethical as she always was wouldn't accept the offer. I on the other hand have no such ethics and was all for grabbing a free holiday while the going was good. Pam won.

A year or two later when we had both retired I brought up the question of this free trip again and now that it was 'ethical', Pam had no such inhibitions and agreed it was a possibility. She had the telephone number of her ex-client but still felt it a bit of a cheek and was reluctant to make the call and ask if the offer was still good. As I have said, inhibitions are the last thing I have and reminding someone that they had offered me a free holiday wasn't a strain on my conscience whatsoever. I duly made the call.

The ex-client not only remembered the offer but was most enthusiastic, very enthusiastic actually and I was immediately suspicious. I agreed to meet him at his business premises in Kent to get the details. He ran a second-hand car business and I have never heard yet of anyone in that business who was honest or didn't have his finger in some nefarious pie or other. He more or less confirmed what I thought when he casually mentioned if, whilst I was there I could hand over several thousand pounds to someone who would come around for it!! He said he would also throw in a hire car for nothing as I was really doing him a favour. I don't know if he thought I had just come up the river on a banana boat but for a free holiday I was prepared to be a schmuck. We sorted out the various details and I went home to give Pam the good news about our free holiday, omitting the bit about the money. She really was too innocent and honest to be troubled by such mundane things.

The day duly arrived and off we went for our holiday. We landed in Alicante and quickly found the car rental place and the car which had been reserved for us, all very nice. He hadn't exactly gone overboard on the size of car he had reserved for us. In fact it was one of those things routinely described as 'compact', but I call them bloody small. Being over six feet tall and owning a Landrover Discovery probably had something to do with my jaundiced view on 'compact' cars.

With Pam navigating we duly arrived at the villa complex just south of Benidorm. It was after midnight when we arrived. There wasn't any street lighting and the only impression of the place was that the villa was at the top of a very steep hill which ran down into a cul-de sac. I parked the car, left it in gear and prayed the handbrake worked properly. We grabbed our cases and went to explore the villa before going to bed. In actual fact it was a very nice place indeed. As well as being tastefully decorated it had every mod-con imaginable.

Every room, and there were several, was fitted out to a very high standard. We even had new his and hers bath robes. Of course there was the obligatory SKY television with about half a million channels to choose from. I thought this was just the ticket for a couple of weeks in the sun. Quite content, we had something to drink and went to bed both falling asleep quickly after a fairly hectic day.

"Hello". The sun was just lighting the sky when again I heard someone calling "Hello". I gave Pam a nudge and told her someone was at the door, hoping she would get up and sort it out. Nothing doing, she muttered something about not speaking Spanish and so I got up to answer the call only then realising I didn't speak bloody Spanish either and not only that the "Hello" was very much in English. I put on one of the luxurious bathrobes and headed for the door. The "Hellos" were getting more frantic by the second and I wondered what was so pressing. I thought perhaps it was the chap coming to collect the money I had brought over and was getting a bit impatient.

I opened the door and.... No one there! I then heard a "Hello" from the side of the villa and walked around but again no one there. Another "Hello" from the back and so off I went but again no one was there. Getting somewhat pissed off at being dragged out of bed at an ungodly hour and then having to pursue some cretin around the place I quickly did a tour of the villa with a view to giving someone a rollicking. I did a complete tour of the place and still found no one. I couldn't understand it, particularly as I had heard yet another "Hello" just a few seconds before.

I was standing there utterly bemused when there was yet another "Hello" almost beside me which made me jump about six feet in the air! I turned quickly and there sitting on a high post was a bleeding great parrot! I stood staring at this bird for several seconds wondering whether to kill it or not when it cocked its head to one side and said in the most wonderful of English accents, "Good morning, have a nice day" and flew back over the fence from where it had come. It turned out it belonged to an English ex-pat living next door who had taught it all sorts of things. Obviously the bird was quite content and never wondered off. Pam had heard all of these exchanges whilst lying in bed and when I told her it was a parrot wondered if I had made an early start on the Sangria. The bird actually belonged to Stuart Hall of 'It's a Knockout' fame. I was all for going around to ask for his autograph and generally suck up to him. I thought he was magnificent on that program. Pam, on the other hand, hated his guts so I had to content myself with the occasional glimpse of my hero.

Having made an early start to the day because of the parrot I decided to stay up and make breakfast for us both, Pam and I, not the parrot! It was while we were having breakfast that our second visitor turned up in the form of an English lad who said he had come to collect the package I had brought out. He felt the need to explain that the money was for doing 'odd jobs' and that he didn't have a bank account! Pam didn't know what he was talking about as I still hadn't told her about the several thousand we had brought over in the suitcase. After he had gone she asked me what it was all about and I simply brushed it off as a favour to her client and that it was only a small amount. She gave me a look that spoke volumes but decided not to pursue it. She knew that sometimes I stretched the odd point and that it was best just not to know the detail! Anyway I hadn't done anything illegal, I think!

Having finished breakfast it was time to do some shopping. I hadn't even signed for the car and it was arranged that someone from the company would be calling around sometime in the afternoon to check my licence and fill out the necessary documents, all very Spanish! I told Pam we could easily do the shopping and be back sunbathing around the pool long before the chap came to complete the formalities. As usual she trusted me and agreed.

I have already said that I had parked the car facing down a very steep hill which led into the cul-de-sac of the villa complex. We got into the car and looking down the hill, about two hundred metres away at the furthest point of the cul-de sac was a man washing a rather magnificent Mercedes Benz in front of his villa. I started the car and because we were facing down the hill I let off the handbrake with the intention of rolling down the hill to the dead end and then engaging gear to 'bump start'; and then drive out the way we had come. Once the hand brake was off the car shot forward as if someone had kicked it! The chap cleaning his car stopped what he was doing to watch us hurtle towards him and I felt Pam stiffen with apprehension at the speed at which we were descending.

About two thirds of the way down I decided that I had better slow the car as we really were flying by now. I put my foot on the brake....Nothing! I stamped repeatedly on the pedal but nothing happened. The chap cleaning his Mercedes just stood there open mouthed as we barrelled towards him. We flew into the cul-de-sac at a tremendous speed and out of the corner of my eye I saw Pam prepare for the inevitable with feet and arms firmly braced. At the last moment, and in utter desperation, I jerked the steering wheel to the right to avoid the Mercedes and flew onto the drive of the adjacent villa. Had I been able to I would probably have shouted something like "fucking hell" because there, parked on the drive was yet another bloody great Mercedes but in truth I was too petrified to say anything. Still stamping like mad on the brake pedal I again jerked the steering wheel to the right to avoid it and promptly shot over an adjacent low level wall with a resounding crash as the front of our, as of yet, not properly documented hire car parked its nose on the corner of the villa!

We both sat there slightly dazed at how quickly this had all happened and fortunately neither of us were hurt. The car had finally come to a stop precariously balanced on the low-level wall with its nose touching the villa, but what now troubled me was that if the balance was upset the bloody car could fall off the wall and down into a rather deep basement. I told Pam not to move and it seemed like a long time but must have only been seconds before people appeared from everywhere. Fortunately a good number of them were very large and turned out to be Dutch and Germans. They quickly grasped the situation and before we knew it had dragged the car back, literally, from the precipice!

Once calm had returned and our nerves had settled I checked out the car, particularly the brakes! It was then I discovered, to my eternal embarrassment that there was nothing wrong with the brakes! Because the car was a compact car and I was used to driving a bloody great Landrover the configuration of the pedals was much closer than I was used to and I had in fact been stamping on the clutch pedal all the way down the hill. I checked out the rest of the car and surprisingly there was very little damage. The underneath was knocked about quite a lot, but there was nothing leaking and the engine still worked so thanking everyone profusely and promising to let the insurance company have the details of the damage to the villa, we made our fond farewell!

Pam was all for going back to the villa as her confidence in my driving had taken a definite dive! I convinced her that we still needed to go to the supermarket for food and that as we were out, what on earth else could possibly happen!! We drove to the supermarket and parked in a bay which was situated in almost the middle of a huge and virtually empty car park. About fifty metres away and at right angles to us was parked a rather large Peugeot. As Pam was gathering her things a couple got into the car and I casually watched as the reversing lights came on and the car shot backward at high speed. I just couldn't believe what I knew was going to happen. It reversed across the fifty metres at high speed and with an almighty crash slammed into the side of our still undocumented and unregistered hire car. Glass and bits of metal flew everywhere and when the crazy sod that was driving the Peugeot pulled forward the rear bumper also fell off! I didn't know whether I should laugh or cry. Pam whose nerves were already somewhat frayed just sat there in stunned silence. It turned out it was another hire car and an automatic which the driver was just not used to. Having swapped even more insurance details, most of which I was making up as I went along, we completed our shopping and made our way back, very carefully, to the villa. The chap duly arrived to get me to sign the documents and hardly glanced at the car, which was just as well I thought. I told Pam I would square it all up with her ex client when we got back to the U.K. and not to worry!!

Needless to say whenever we went out in the car Pam was a nervous wreck and so we spent rather a lot of time either walking in the hills or sitting around the pool. There never were any repercussions about the car. I put it down to the fact that we had done Pam's client a favour with regards the money I took over and he was content to let things be. It really was a most remarkable start to any holiday we had ever been on and fortunately was never repeated.

THE EUSTON SPIDER

One of the oldest practical jokes in the world must be the dropping of a fake spider or some equally obnoxious thing onto someone and watching them jump. Firemen were especially good at refining these jokes and so it came to pass that the Euston Spider entered Brigade folklore.

I was serving at Fulham Fire Station, having been turfed out of training school but that's another story!! Being at Fulham wasn't too bad but I wanted to get back to Euston if I could. I was in regular contact with the O.I.C. on one of the watches at Euston who had promised me that should a vacancy occur he would let me know before anyone else had the chance to apply. Eventually it came to pass that a vacancy did occur on my old watch and I promptly applied for and obtained the posting. This is the tale of how that vacancy came about!

Euston Fire Station, situated as it is on Euston Road, has thousands of people passing it every hour and even at night there is always a steady trickle of people walking by. Euston road is never quiet.

It was decided by the Officer in Charge (later to become a Senior Officer in the Brigade!) that a boring night shift was to be livened up by having a fake spider drop on people as they walked by the station. All very responsible and adult I hear you say. There happens to be a huge plane tree on the pavement outside the station and its branches were perfect for running a line over one of them with the spider attached. The line was run back into the station where the men waited for a suitable victim to walk by, when the spider would then be plopped down on their head or shoulders.

I had performed a very similar trick at Kensington but with a large soggy cloth I named the 'Rat'. It is most gratifying to see people leap in the air with fright, infantile

I grant you, but still very gratifying. Anyway the spider at Euston was ready and as night fell and the numbers of people passing slowed, the wheeze was put into play.

The spider was quite realistic, well realistic if you are a fan of horror films that is! Very large and hairy with enormous legs. Selecting a victim wasn't too scientific. Women were always the best target as they reacted superbly. You could invariably count on a window-breaking scream from a woman. Men though were often targeted, but for obvious reasons not the ones who looked as if they could do ten rounds with Mike Tyson!

The trick really was to keep the joke in play for as long as possible. Sometimes the spider would be dropped just in front of someone and as they tried to avoid it so it would be pulled and jerked so that it appeared to be chasing them. Some of the antics were a joy to behold. Victims would leap up and down and some would actually go back the way they had come rather than risk being bitten. Some would become entangled in the line and would become absolutely panic-stricken at the feel of something around their legs, particularly as the spider, because of the line attached to their legs, now appeared to chase them as they ran.

Most people, when they realised they had been tricked, took it in good part. A few needed their ruffled feathers smoothing when they felt their dignity had been offended but generally it was a lot of fun; until something went wrong!

The next victim to come along was a middle-aged woman. It was decided to try to drop the spider directly onto her rather than near her in the hope that the reaction would be worth seeing. In this the Firemen's hopes were more than realised. As the woman walked under the tree the spider was dropped with unerring accuracy straight on to her head and then rolled down over her face and on to her chest. The initial result was perfect, a very loud scream and lots of jumping about. It was the subsequent event which caused a problem! The women had a weak heart and promptly had a heart attack and collapsed in a heap on the pavement!

For a second or two there was much hilarity in the Fire Station, but it was soon realised that something serious had happened and the men rushed out to try to make amends. First aid and resuscitation were given and the woman was kept alive until an ambulance arrived to take her to hospital.

The woman remained in a critical condition for some time but fortunately made a complete recovery. The Officer in Charge was fortunate not to lose his job. He was given an almighty rollicking and kicked out of Euston to a desk job somewhere. He did eventually become a very senior officer in the Brigade which really does prove the old adage that any publicity is good publicity! It was this vacancy which I applied for and filled. As for the woman, I can only assume the Brigade came to some arrangement with her as I never heard any more about it. I was also no longer tempted to drop spiders or anything else on members of the public.

GRATITUDE

Euston like most of London is full of council flats, hotels and shops. In this modern era it also has its full quota of coffee shops and 'up market' stores and most of the people in the area now seem to be from eastern Europe either serving the coffee or making the fast food! Certainly not the Euston I knew and grew up in.

Back in the 70s when I was stationed there it was still very much 'original' London. Just down the Euston Road towards Kings Cross was an area frequented by the many prostitutes in the area, the hotels used to let the rooms by the hour and at all hours of the day and night the drunks and drug addicts wandered about, a nice place.

There were also many blocks of council flats mainly in the back streets and dating back to before the war, the Second World War that is! It was to one of these blocks we were called one Saturday afternoon. When we arrived it was obvious there was a serious fire in one of the flats on an upper floor.

The crews are trained to respond to almost any given situation in a semi-automatic way. It's the reason the Brigade drill so much. Time is of the utmost essence in an emergency and quite obviously, if orders had to be given in detail then that would take time and perhaps lives lost.

Whilst the crew got to work running out hose, donning breathing apparatus and a dozen other tasks I made a quick 'recce' to the flat on fire. Being the Officer in Charge I needed to be able to make some sort of assessment and direct the crews as they arrived.

The front door to the flat was wide open and so I crawled in under the smoke and found myself in a long corridor and could see the fire blazing at the end in a bedroom. That the fire was so fierce wasn't such a bad thing as the generated heat was keeping the smoke from totally filling the hallway.

I decided to make my way to the bedroom to do a quick check to see if anyone was involved. I crawled into the room and was mildly surprised to see a body lying beside the bed. By now the room was blazing and the heat and smoke building up badly, so without any finesse at all I grabbed a pair of legs and started dragging the body out of the room and along the passage.

By the time I arrived at the front door other Fireman had arrived and helped me carry, what turned out to be, a very elderly lady, quite obviously suffering from smoke inhalation but remarkably few burns, to fresh air.

Once out on the balcony and in the open, we laid her down and I started checking her vital signs. As I touched her throat to check for a pulse her eyes sprung open and she fixed me with a glare and in a cockney accent that equaled my own shouted at me to 'fuck off'! For once in my life I was speechless. I knelt there for a few seconds before she yet again told me to 'Fuck off'. I'm quite used to people behaving strangely, stress does that to them, but she seemed fully in control of herself which made her outburst even more bizarre. As she was quite obviously not at death's door, I left her in the care of a Fireman and eventually she was taken to hospital by ambulance.

I never saw her again but as I always had reports to file, it was necessary to ascertain if she in fact had survived, the extent of her injuries etc. I found out she was in her 80s and she did indeed make a full recovery. Saving a life is the most satisfying thing anyone could possibly do and I was fortunate to have done so on several occasions but without a doubt I have never been told to 'fuck off' whilst doing it!! That was a first!!

A NASTY SMELL IN THE TOILET

If it was going to happen anywhere, it was going to happen at Euston Fire Station. Most of my tomfoolery and funny experiences happened at Euston. It was as if the most extrovert Firemen in the Brigade gravitated there. Or it was perhaps the policy of Senior Officers to put most of their 'nutters' in one basket, who knows? Situated as it is, on the Euston Road, one of the busiest roads in Europe and between the main line railway stations of Euston, St Pancras and Kings Cross, the Fire Station was always bubbling with an expectation that something was going to happen. The vast hordes of football supporters always made a point of hurling abuse and a few empty beer cans our way on their trips to and from football grounds. Of the hundreds of thousands of commuters who passed by daily, some would always be knocking on the door with some question or problem. By and large we never minded. After all we were there to serve the public. I suppose we appeared as some sort of Samaritans or D.I.Y service.

Most of the people who live in the area are decent and hardworking. Unfortunately there are a lot of dross also; drug addicts, prostitutes and their pimps, some of the lowest forms of life you could ever be unfortunate to come across. I was born in the area and lived there until I was twenty-one and I eventually served over ten years there as both Fireman and Officer, so I know it intimately. This low life gravitates towards a Fire Station like a moth to a bright light. When you return from a fire, cold and wet, in the middle of the night in winter it was always possible to find one of these stinking bastards snoozing in your bed. I'm afraid the caring and loving side of your personality goes right out of the window. The darker side of a Fireman's nature tends to take over and the offending person is likely to be ejected, in short, slung out by the scruff of his neck. So much for a place of sanctuary and a benevolent attitude! I believed then, and still do, that there is nothing to be done with these people. The more you give, the more they want. Sod that! Not to say we felt that way with everyone. On the odd occasion the price of a meal would be given but that was rare. We knew it would just be spent on booze or drugs.

Because of the strange and the weird people who are attracted to Fire Stations (Firemen included!) the cardinal rule is; 'Under no circumstances allow a member of the public on the station at any time without an escort'. Apart from thieving from locker rooms and damaging anything they have a mind to, members of the public have been known to attack and seriously injure Firemen, and on one occasion actually kill a member of the Brigade. Mind you, he was knocking off the bloke's missus so it was probably justified!! It was because this rule was ignored that the tale that follows occurred. Fortunately it was a Fireman on the Green Watch (I was White Watch) who committed the first mistake, thus saving me from about a year's worth of paperwork.

It was during a day duty that the front door bell rang and Woody (yep, another nickname, just like on the telly) answered it. Standing on the forecourt was a wide-eyed black teenager. Having politely been asked by Woody what he wanted, the teenager asked if he could use the toilet. A perfectly normal occurrence at a fire station I can assure you! The equally normal reply would be a standard "Fuck off"! For some reason that nobody has ever understood, least of all Woody, he actually said yes and let the lad into the station. Taking him to the nearest toilet, which was situated at the back of the appliance (fire engine) bay. There he left him, instructing him to let himself out when he had finished. Woody then went back to work and thought no more about it.

We took over from the Green Watch that night and carried out the various duties which were necessary to maintain the appliances etc. At that time we used to have an evening meal at 8 p.m., after which there was a stand down period when the members of the Watch, providing there was no essential work, could please themselves as to what they did. That particular evening, most gravitated towards the television room but about ten of us decided, as usual, to play a game of five-a-side football in the appliance room. The appliances were driven on to the forecourt and the cavernous appliance bay instantly converted to a perfect football field. We played for a couple of hours and during that time the odd player needed to visit the toilet that was situated at the back of the appliance bay. Finding it locked, they used another toilet elsewhere on the station. It registered with me that the appliance bay toilet was locked and I assumed it was defective and that the Green Watch had completed the necessary paperwork for its repair. Wrong!

The next morning the Red Watch took over from us, and that evening we again took over from them to start our second night shift. As I have already explained, once our duties and evening meal were finished, we would once again park the appliances on the forecourt and play football. Not a bad life really. The toilet was still locked; only this time when I was told this news by a 'bursting' fireman, he added "and it fucking stinks!" I reminded him that is what toilets normally do and to stop sodding about, find another one so we could get on with the bloody game. Several of the watch did in fact report to me that the smell was pretty bad but there was nothing to be done until the next day. I simply assumed the smell had something to do with the 'defective' toilet. Again at 0900 hours the next morning the Red Watch took over from us and we went off duty, not giving the toilet a second thought.

The Officer in Charge of the Red Watch was a singularly unlucky man. He was at Euston, on loan as it were from Soho Fire Station. He was an extremely capable and experienced Officer and well liked by his men, but unlucky! For example, just a few weeks earlier he had attended a fire in one of the many seedier hotels around Euston and he and his men had done a good job. Unfortunately, after they had left the scene, a cleaner had gone into the apartment to clean and upon entering the bathroom had found an asphyxiated body lying in the bath! Now the Senior Officers in the Brigade take a very dim view of us leaving dead bodies around (Apparently the cleaner had such a fright she nearly dropped dead as well) and our luckless O.I.C. was fortunate not to face disciplinary action.

During the course of his watch, the O.I.C also received complaints from his men about the smell from the toilet, which was still out of service and stank like hell. Trying desperately to now appear efficient, he checked the paperwork in order to find out when the toilet had been reported defective (something I should have done!!) and when it was to be repaired. Finding that it hadn't been reported, he ordered one of his men to climb over an adjoining wall; the two toilets were separated by a wall that extended high enough to afford privacy but didn't extend very high, and to open the door to discover what the defect was. The Fireman concerned climbed the wall and peered down, looking for a place to land. That was as far as he got. Muttering a cry of "Fucking hell!" he jumped back down and rushed to the office to inform his Guvnor that there was a body hanging by its neck in the toilet. Now it is well known that a Fireman's sense of humour is a little strange. To the general public it would seem cruel and macabre, but to other Firemen perfectly reasonable. Our luckless O.I.C. thought another wind-up was in progress, but the man's insistence prevailed so he reluctantly ordered that the door be forced open.

There, hanging by his neck from the toilet cistern, was the teenager Woody had let into the station several days earlier. No wonder it stank! Thinking "Why me?", the Guvnor set in motion the wheels of officialdom. The police were called as well as our own Senior Officers. The enquiry that followed reached a conclusion that merely confirmed what we all knew: that the teenager had gone into the toilet and hanged himself! What else?

Unfortunately for the Station Officer he was to suffer harassment from the dead boy's family for a long time after. They would come around to the station and hold small demonstrations, accusing him of murdering the boy. Several times the police had to be called, since it appeared the Fire Station was about to be stormed and personnel assaulted. The wisecracks and jokes surrounding this event went on for months. "Strange way to flush a toilet!", "Dying for a shit!", "Dead ringer for someone" etc. etc. There was no end to them. As is the way with humour in the Brigade, I was accused of knowing there was a body in the toilet and of completely ignoring it over two nights because I didn't want to do the paperwork that would be involved. Not the slightest truth in that accusation at all! Eventually the demonstrations and paperwork stopped and would you believe the luckless O.I.C. was eventually promoted. Where to? Euston, where else?

GUARD DUTY

Paul Atwell or 'Atters' as he came to be known joined the station straight from Training School. Although a most personable man and liked immediately by everyone, this wasn't going to stop the watch from having some fun at his expense. Making life awkward for new recruits was, and probably still is, a time-honoured tradition in any service. I have no doubt that many consider this 'fun' simply as bullying and in some cases it probably is. The difference is in the degree or persistent nature of the fun. There is a line and when it is overstepped, then it does become bullying; the trick is to not let things get out of hand.

Because recruits are ignorant as to routines on a station almost anything that is said to them they believe, particularly if it is the Officer in Charge saying it. After Paul had been with the watch for a couple of shifts one of the men came up with the idea of getting him to mount a guard outside the station. It wasn't too difficult to do as at the time the I.R.A. were running a bombing campaign all over the U.K. and London had already had several attacks so guarding a fire station, on the face of it, wasn't too ridiculous.

To give it some degree of credibility I had typed an 'order' from Brigade Headquarters that information had been received from the police that a terrorist attack was going to be mounted on a Fire Station in London and we were to provide our own security by patrolling both inside and outside the station. I gathered the watch and called for volunteers. Someone immediately volunteered to mount a guard inside and then there was a pause as I waited for a volunteer to patrol around the outside of the station.

It was Atters who of course was embarrassed into volunteering. All it took were a few pointed looks in his direction and he couldn't do anything else. Just as planned.

Then to give the story added credibility I called for further volunteers to relieve these two later on and then others to provide further reliefs during the night. I briefed the men on what was required and everyone kept a straight face. Paul looked terrified at the prospect of so much responsibility and his discomfort only added to our somewhat perverted pleasure.

They were to wear full firefighting uniform complete with axe which was for protection should there be a terrorist attack! I haven't mentioned that of course there most definitely was going to be a terrorist attack. And so Atters, suitably attired and as nervous as hell, was despatched to the pavement in Euston Road at nine o'clock at night to begin his patrol of the station. You might think some people are just plain gullible but remember these poor buggers just didn't have a clue as to what was expected of them and were prime targets for a practical joke.

The plan now was for one of the Fireman to dress up as a terrorist. Not having any idea what a terrorist looked like we simply picked the nastiest looking man on the watch and dressed him in a raincoat and cloth cap and blackened his face with dirt. Vernon Sharp was the name of the 'terrorist' and a villainous looking bastard he was too! In fact Vernon was knifed to death the following year in a bar fight! We had obviously picked the right one to play a terrorist.

We let Paul do a couple of circuits of the station just to settle in. His orders were to raise the alarm if he saw anything suspicious and tackle anyone trespassing on the station. Vernon slipped out with the hat pulled down low to give shadow to his face and carrying a box which of course concealed a 'bomb', and started tracking Paul around the block. Euston Fire Station is in effect on an island, a road running all the way around its boundary, so it is possible to walk around the whole Fire Station without leaving the pavement.

As Paul completed a circuit, arriving back at the front on Euston Road, Vernon appeared as if from nowhere and ran on to the station forecourt and placed the bomb by the appliance doors. It was impossible for Atters not to see this but obviously deciding that discretion was the better part of valour, ignored it completely. The whole watch, who were hiding behind various windows, saw this act of 'bravery' and were greatly disappointed that Paul hadn't reacted in a more suitable way. Vernon, who was still crouched by the bomb presumably fusing the bloody thing, also saw that Atters was cocking a deaf'un! Not to be in any way thwarted by our reluctant security guard, Vernon picked up the bomb and ran across the forecourt to place it by the fuel pumps. He did this virtually under the nose of Paul and this time he couldn't ignore it. Now things really got going and the result was something we hadn't counted on. We thought that Paul would simply challenge him and that the whole thing would fizzle out with Paul realising he had been had. Instead he drew his axe and attempted to pin Vernon to the ground. Vernon kept the game going by resisting and throwing Paul off and ran off the forecourt and onto Euston Road followed by Paul shouting and hollering.

It just so happened that a man was walking his large Alsatian dog by the station when Vernon came running out followed by a fireman screaming for help. This denizen of law and order immediately sized up the situation and promptly set his dog on to Vernon. The dog, not being party to the joke, set to with a vengeance and sank its teeth into various parts of Vernon's anatomy. Paul still screaming and shouting about bombs and terrorists was attracting quite a crowd. Amongst which was a burly taxi driver who had stopped his cab when he saw what was happening and when told it was a terrorist joined in and started punching and kicking him. Vernon was desperately trying to explain that it was a joke but between the dog biting him and the cab driver trying to cripple him found it impossible. In fact he was almost fighting for his life.

This all happened within seconds and at first we couldn't believe the bloody mayhem that had been unleashed just outside the station. I half expected to see a rope thrown across a lamp post and Vernon hung by his neck! Half the watch were for Vernon to be left to his fate, such is the black humour of Firemen. I, on the other hand would have a lot of explaining to do if one of my men were to be hospitalised, or worse, by a mob growing bigger by the minute who were pissed off by Irishmen planting bombs and were intent on exacting revenge, payback time.

I rushed out with a couple of other Firemen and as quickly as possible calmed the situation. Vernon, by now needing first aid, was glad to be rescued. The cab driver and dog owner I placated by telling them it was a security exercise and that I would be recommending them for their public-spirited response, the best bit of bullshit I could think of at the time. The dog was still not in on the joke and continued to try and take lumps out of anyone within biting distance and this gave us a good excuse to hurriedly extract ourselves leaving several bemused members of the public standing on the pavement.

I was glad to be back in the station as I could see that this joke had great potential for getting me the sack, not that anyone would have cared of course. Fortunately the police had not turned up, which was quite unusual. They would definitely not have been amused. In the past they had cautioned us that one day we would overstep the mark.

Fortunately all ended well and Paul 'Atters' Atwell having finally realised he had been 'had' joined in the laughter and was now a fully fledged and initiated member of the watch. Vernon was roundly commended by all for his acting and, apart from a few bruises and bites from the dog and copious amounts of antiseptics wasn't too badly hurt. He was a natural for play acting and also for getting himself into trouble. He caused me all sorts of problems from time to time but oddly we got on very well. I have to say though that I wasn't too surprised to hear he had been stabbed and killed in a bar fight.

LURCH'S CHEESE SANDWICH

We called Colin 'Lurch' for no other reason than it rhymed with his surname, Birch. Behaving stupidly was normal for Colin and in fact he was as near a lunatic as you can be without being certified. He would be involved in every prank which occurred on the station and often working entirely alone would pull some stunt that ended with someone getting wet or worse! With Colin, being a pain in the arse was a full-time occupation and he excelled at it.

It has to be said though that he was tolerated because, although when on the station he drove everyone crazy from the Guvnor to the lowliest Fireman, he had several attributes that made him a credit to the Fire Service and a valuable member of the watch. Whenever 'the bells went down' he was transformed into one of the best Firemen I have ever met. His topographical knowledge was legendary as was his driving ability. He handled those several ton monsters as if they were go-carts, often scaring rigid those who didn't know how good a driver he was. His work rate at a fire was incredible and I have seen him in a near state of collapse several times. He also had a personality and character which was extremely affable and despite being a bloody nuisance was well liked by everyone.

He was tall and skinny and in fact there was more fat on a chip than was on his body. He had a prodigious appetite which made no difference at all to his size as he remained tall and skinny his entire career. At meal times he would be first in the queue and would eat as if he had never seen food before, throwing it down as if in some sort of competition. Often there would be food put on the table which was surplus from the meal and he would grab it before anyone else and with no thought of sharing or offering.

At 'stand easy' (tea break) a cheese sandwich with lots of onions with a cup of tea was standard fare for all. The mess manager would make the sandwiches and usually there would be one or two spares, which were made from the surplus cheese. Lurch, because he would have swallowed his sandwich without it touching the side of his gullet, would then grab a spare and wolf that down as well. It meant of course that it was a very rare stand easy, when someone other than Lurch managed to eat a spare ''sarnie'.

It was decided that Colin needed to be taught a lesson with regards behaving like a pig in a trough. Because he was so greedy it wasn't too difficult. Once the mess manager had made the sandwiches for the watch (crews) he made a spare sandwich which he set by the side of the main pile as the 'spare'. The slight difference with this sandwich was that the cheese hanging out of the side of the sandwich was the only cheese; the main body of the sandwich was made up of carbolic soap!

The whole watch knew about the special sandwich, with of course Lurch being the exception. Stand easy is at 11 o'clock and as usual Colin was first in the mess grabbing his sandwich and cup of tea and eyeing up the spare sandwich while stuffing the first one into his mouth. In what seemed like record time he had finished and grabbed the spare almost before the rest of the watch had made a start.

Without a pause he started munching his way through the carbolic soap sandwich and to a man the rest of the watch stopped what they were doing and watched. It was a matter of some amazement to us that he had worked his way through about half the sandwich before something began to register on his taste buds. It was a tribute to his concentration and greedy nature regarding food that he didn't notice us watching him swallow the soapy sandwich. We were all probably wishing he would explode in a cloud of bubbles or start foaming at the mouth!

At last his brain caught up with his greed as the carbolic soap assaulted his throat and stomach! The shifting expressions on his face were most gratifying. First there was a look of bafflement, followed by confusion and then a realisation of what had happened. He started to splutter and heave as the taste worked its way up and down his digestive system. It was an absolute pleasure for us to watch and it never troubled any of us that we might have actually poisoned him. Such was the pleasure of seeing someone get their just dessert, or in this case, their just cheese sandwich!

Another second or two passed and the need to vomit was too great. He made a rapid exit from the mess heading for the nearest toilet and to our collective satisfaction vomited copiously! Unsurprisingly perhaps he felt quite ill for several hours and turned a slight greenish colour, much to everyone's amusement. Did it cure him of his pig-like tendencies? No, of course not but it gave us some satisfaction and slowed him down at meal times, well at least for a week or two!

Waiting to take my crew into an underground fire at Harrods. Note the Breathing apparatus. This set, with just a few moderations, was in use a hundred years ago! It has now been superseded by air sets but they can only keep you alive for around thirty minutes. The oxygen set that I'm wearing could keep you alive for several hours.

'THE PHANTOM'

Life on a fire station is not all drills, lectures or rushing around the streets in Fire Engines with sirens howling. Quite often it can be tedious and even boring. At times, when life is somewhat monotonous, it is the personnel with their differing characters and personalities who make life on a station tolerable and entertaining. But without the stimulus of fires or other emergencies even these diverse characters, after a few weeks of no action, tend to become morose and discontented. It is the job of the Officer in Charge not only to lead his men on the fire ground but also to fill their day with constructive work. Even so, after a few weeks of filling the day with drills, lectures, fire prevention work etc., even the most conscientious of Officers are scratching around for something original and stimulating for their men to do.

It was during one of these slack periods that the Phantom was born. I was stationed at Euston and as the Deputy in Charge was more often than not charged with giving the men drills etc. Whilst I was actively engaged, the Guvnor attended to matters of great importance, usually with his feet up in front of the council-issue gas fire and a cup of coffee in his hand. There are only a couple of hundred different drills that can be given as well as a few thousand variations and over the years we had gone through them countless times. I was as fed up as the rest of the Watch. They had to listen to me bawling and shouting orders and more and more often giving them bollockings because they were getting sloppy at their work. In fairness to the men, they were very good at their job, but the fire `famine` was having an insidious effect on morale. Drastic action was needed!

I was off duty and doing some shopping when I passed one of those joke shops. You know, the ones that sell horror masks and magic kits. Standing in front of the shop window, an idea was born. Ten minutes later I was back out on the street, the owner of a mask and a couple of cans of spray `string`. The mask was magnificent. It was the face of an incredibly old man with heavy wrinkles and long white hair. When I arrived back home, I found an old white sheet that made a perfect shroud. Putting the mask and shroud on, I tried it out on my son. He was only seven years old and it frightened the life out of him. Just perfect for a fire station then! I couldn`t wait for my next night shift.

The shift system eventually placed our watch on nights and I waited as patiently as I could for the watch to turn in. As usual, there were a few who sat up until the early hours playing cards or just talking but eventually, about two or three o'clock in the morning, the whole watch was asleep and the station as quiet as a cemetery! I had selected my first 'victim' simply because he slept alone in one of the downstairs rooms next to the Fire Engines. He was a Leading Fireman and a brave leader of men at that! I donned the mask and shroud, crept out of my quarters on the first floor of the station, and started to descend the stairs. Passing a window on the way I managed to make myself jump as the reflection of this horrible figure glared at me. Giggling at my own stupidity, I crept on down the stairs. Only by the faint glow of the street lights filtering in through the windows was I able to find my way without falling arse over head. After a few minutes I arrived at the door to the Leading Fireman's room.

I was alternately shaking with the giggles and sweating with the thought that I was liable to get 'filled in' if I were to be caught. Not to mention my credibility as an Officer going right out of the window! I eased open the door and by the light filtering in from the street made out the Leading Fireman, fast asleep, his chest gently rising and falling and obviously at peace with the world. I wedged open the door to allow for a quick exit, and switched on the light. Nothing. He didn't budge at all. I could have stood there all night. He was out cold. The Phantom was certainly not going to put up with this. Measures were called for!

I pulled from beneath the shroud the can of spray 'string' and came within a foot or two from his face – a dodgy thing to do as things could turn violent but I had no choice, the bastard was going to sleep forever! As I reached down to touch him something deep down in his slumbering brain must have occurred and his eyes sprung open. The effect was astounding. I could see all sorts of horrors reflected in his face as his brain tried desperately to adjust. A split second passed in which I just stood there dressed like the Grim Reaper. It never occurred to me that the poor bastard could have had a heart attack!! He then let out an ear-piercing scream and yanked the blankets over his head, continuing all the while to scream. I was standing there wondering what to do next when the muffled screams changed to shouts of 'NO!' 'NO!' 'NO!' and he whipped back the blankets as if to confirm in some way that he was just having a nightmare. Unfortunately for him, the nightmare continued. No sooner had his face reappeared than I let him have it with the can of spray string straight into his face. Again his reaction was a joy to see, and hear! The plastic string was all over his face, in his mouth and eyes and he was spluttering like a baby! With the physical effect of now being covered in this messy stuff, I could see some sort of sanity returning. It was time for the Phantom to make his getaway and quick too, as this man had a reputation for a quick temper and was powerfully built.

I ran from his room and returned upstairs to my own quarters, disrobing as I went, dived into my own bed and tucked the shroud and mask along with the tin of plastic string down under the blankets. and tried desperately to stifle the laughter and tears. As I lay there, I heard a tremendous row going on downstairs. I thought it prudent not to go and see as I doubted I could keep a straight face and give the game away. Come the next morning I found out that the Leading Fireman believed it was one of the Firemen, who had pulled this stunt, and he had woken everyone up and got them out of their beds, threatening them with just about everything and anything. That was a little bonus I certainly hadn't reckoned on.

The whole watch roused out of their beds and given a bollocking, fabulous! This little episode kept the watch speculating as to the identity of the Phantom, but some of them were still unconvinced that the event had actually occurred, believing instead that the Leading Fireman himself had pulled a stunt on them by dragging them out of bed. They would come to believe that the 'Phantom' was real alright! As well as my can of spray 'string' I would soon have a box of custard pies from the joke shop and intended to use them!

I thought it wise to let a few weeks pass and let things settle down. After a few weeks I thought it was about time the Phantom made another nocturnal foray. The watch had finally settled down and had more or less forgotten about the first 'visit'. My modus operandi remained essentially the same, only this time I decided to use a custard pie. I decided that a visit to the men's locker room, where about six of them would be sleeping, was worth a visit. The risks were huge of course. It would only take one of them to be awake and all would be lost. I couldn't expect any mercy if I were to be caught! Reaching the locker room, I entered by the swing doors that led from the appliance room. Again I was met by the comforting sounds of something akin to a pigpen, snoring and grunting and restless movement. I was sweating heavily. This business was turning me into a nervous wreck. I crept up to the nearest Fireman again beginning to giggle to myself like an idiot, my silly giggling probably added quite well to the overall effect. This one, unlike the first one, didn't wake up and so I had to give him a shake. His eyes snapped open and, seeing this apparition a couple of feet away, he opened his mouth to scream. Before he could do so, I smacked the custard pie full into his face and ran like hell. As I ran I added to the bedlam unfolding by screaming something about the devil or some similar nonsense. Pandemonium broke out behind me. With me screaming and the unfortunate victim dripping custard pie and still hollering and shouting, the entire watch was awake and wondering what the hell was going on. I of course was back in my bed, giggling like a school kid. At least no one now doubted the existence of the Phantom.

I managed to keep this ridiculous affair going for about a year. The Phantom would not appear for a month or two and then another sortie would frighten the life out of someone else. I sometimes wondered what I would do if one of my victims had had a heart attack. It reached a point that, when we were on the night shift, men would set up traps in various place, some quite lethal, and they had to be told that that sort of thing had to stop or some poor unfortunate sod was going to be killed. Men would sit up all night, afraid of a visitation. From my point of view, the whole business was a huge success. The morale of the watch did pick up, as they now had something to focus on. Speculation was rife as to the identity of the Phantom, but I was never under suspicion. After all, I was the miserable bastard who just kept them drilling and making sure they did their work. It still amazes me that I got away with it for so long. There was a 'spin off' to the exploits of the Phantom. It came in the form of the RETRIBUTER another Fireman acting crazily. One of his exploits is covered in the story THE RETRIBUTER

The end finally came when I applied for and got a transfer to another station. It was time for me to move on. I had been at Euston, off and on, for fifteen years and decided a change was needed. I also thought that the Phantom could make one last and memorable visit. My last night shift there once again saw the Phantom creeping about a darkened station in the middle of the night. This time though it was something akin to a suicide mission, for I was quite prepared to get caught! I had prepared a 'redoubt' in the basement behind the huge gas boiler. I had placed there various types of extinguishers, foam, powder and of course lots of water. I wasn't going to be taken easily!

Arming myself with a foam extinguisher, I first 'hit' the man who was sleeping alone in the watch-room, covering him and his bed with foam. Leaving him spluttering my next stop was the locker room where several more got soaked with the stinking stuff. My cardinal rule up to then had been only to ever surprise one man at a time, now of course I had to hang around a little longer whilst I sprayed everyone in range. As men woke up and others started appearing the cry went up, "THE PHANTOM IS OUT". I retreated to the basement, still dressed as the Phantom and as yet unidentified. I backed myself into the alcove behind the gas boiler and, armed with my pre-positioned extinguishers, prepared to sell myself dearly.

It seemed the whole watch, around twenty or so men, were trying to get at me at once but the foam and powder extinguishers were holding them at bay and it was difficult to actually get me out, I felt like Leonidis at the Battle of Themopylae holding off the Persians!!

After a valiant struggle, I was dragged from my hole and my identity revealed. There were a few gasps of surprise and then they got their revenge. I was stripped naked, tied hand and foot and soaked in stinking foam. They then placed me in the middle of Euston Road with a searchlight trained on me. Eventually a couple of motorists stopped and fearing I might be run over put me on the pavement.

There I lay for several hours, slowly freezing. This was mid-October! Hundreds of people walked past me. After all, this is one of the busiest junctions in the whole of Europe and is never quiet. Even a passing Policeman just gave me a glance and walked on. He obviously knew who had put me there, as the searchlight was still on me. I couldn't believe it. Of all people, it was a bloody wino who eventually set me free. He probably thought I was one of his mates. Anyway, the station had been well and truly locked up and the Firemen simply wouldn't let me back in. I eventually gained access back into the station by scaling the building next door and going over their roof and into the back yard of the station. A burglar couldn't have done it better! That`s Euston for you. It really was the craziest station I had ever served at. The next day I packed my kit and with a bit of a sad heart, left. So ended the reign of the

Phantom. I never set foot in the Fire station again until the year 2018 when I was in the area at a reunion, some 35 years later. I gave them two framed photos dating from around 1904 when the station was built.

As an instructor at the Brigade's Training School, Southwark. In actual fact it was rare for me to wear the full uniform as I was a physical training officer and was usually dressed in a track suit. I was also one of the Brigade's first aid instructors and when giving lectures had to be 'fully booted and spurred'. This was probably one of those times.

THE RETRIBUTER

The Retributer came into being as a direct result of the 'Phantom'. (See previous story) As the Phantom had not, as of yet, been caught one of the Firemen decided he would also invent an alter ego called the Retributer. This Fireman was an ex-naval man and had purloined a set of gunnery anti-flash clothing when leaving the Royal navy. The set consisted of a white anti-flash hood and mask with huge white gauntlets. He also had a large American flag he used as a cape. In this guise, he would patrol the station in an attempt to apprehend and bring to justice the Phantom. Sometimes I did wonder if we were in fact all bloody crazy!

The Retributer invariably confined his antics to the night shift, when he would suddenly burst into a room searching for the Phantom or pounce on someone to check their identity! As I said I did sometimes wonder! The difference between him and the Phantom of course was that everyone knew who he was and his clowning around provided a great deal of amusement.

It came to pass that the Retributer was forced into a day time appearance because his colleagues excluded him from a bit of fun they were having. The morning had passed fairly normally and lunch time arrived. I made my way to the mess room and was surprised to find only one or two of the watch eating so I was immediately suspicious as food usually rates quite high with Firemen. I asked one of the men where the others were but all I got was a non-committal answer, which really put me on alert.

I knew how mad this lot could be and how much trouble they could make if they were not controlled, so I had to know what was going on. I again demanded to know where the rest of the watch were but it was obviously a well-guarded secret. As I sat there finishing my meal, the Leading Fireman sauntered into the mess and gave me a big grin! He picked up a cup of tea and promptly rushed out and back into his room which was adjacent to the mess.

Completely intrigued, I went to his room and found the door locked. This was definitely unusual and obviously something was going on that I wasn't to know about. Knocking on the door and demanding it to be opened elicited a simple 'fuck off'. I was second in command at the time and I could hear the Officer in Charge typing away in the office doing the endless paperwork. If the men were up to something nasty and he found out, there would be hell to pay and it was my job, as his deputy, to ensure the watch ran smoothly. If it didn't, then it reflected on me. No one said life is fair!

Rather than make an issue of it there and then, I ignored the rather blunt advice to go away and simply stood quietly to one side of the door. The Guvnor was still typing away and completely unaware that something was going on. I didn't want to involve him and, whatever was happening, I wanted to deal with it.

After several minutes I heard the door being unlocked and slowly opened. I stood well to one side until a Fireman was half way out and then I grabbed the door to prevent it being closed and forced my way into the room. I was met with a scene that left me absolutely speechless. The O.I.C. was still tapping away on the typewriter and had he seen what I was looking at would have hit the roof!

There lying on the Leading Fireman's bed was a rather attractive blonde stripped completely naked. It was what she was doing that really grabbed the attention! On either side of her stood a Fireman each with his trousers down and she was quite happily masturbating them. Between her wide open legs crouched another Fireman who it seemed was inspecting the area between her legs as if he was searching for something; finally there was another one who seemed intent on moulding her breasts into different shapes!

Oddly enough it was the large black handprints over her torso that drew my attention and intrigued me completely. I subsequently found out she just enjoyed getting dirty! This whole tableau has forever been imprinted on my mind and everyone in the room was now staring at me. The only movement being the girl continuing masturbating the men who, incidentally, were not showing any signs of their ardour flagging! Absolute silence reigned, apart from the 'tap, 'tap, tap' of the boss typing next door. In fact it was the girl who broke the silence when she asked me to go and put on my fire boots, come back and have sex with her! I didn't know if it was my boots or me she fancied but this outrageous scene had to be brought to a conclusion before the Guvnor put in an appearance and charged the bloody lot of us!

I had gathered my thoughts and was just about to restore some sort of sanity when the Retributer made his first and last daytime appearance. As this nutcase had been excluded from the frolics going on with the blonde, he decided that the Retributer needed to obtain some sort of justice. He had got himself dressed up in his kit complete with mask and cape, taken a ladder off one of the fire engines and scaled the outside of the building in Euston Road to the window where the fun was being held; all this in full view of about thirty thousand commuters! He also carried a foam fire extinguisher!

The timing was coincidentally perfect as he had reached the window just as I had forced my way into the room and, just as I was about to assert my rather diminished authority, he crashed the window open and leapt into the room like a raving lunatic. The first one to become covered in foam was the girl who, scared witless by this sudden appearance, started screaming her head off! Several of the men were trying to get out of the door at the same time; others were grappling with the Retributer in an attempt to wrest the extinguisher from him. The result was absolute bedlam!

Having not a hope in hell of sorting this lot out, I felt it prudent that I retreat back into the mess and pretend I was deaf! The Guvnor, roused by the screaming and crashing about, came to find out what the hell was going on. It could only have been a second or two before he arrived that the girl was spirited away to another part of the station and he never found out about her. I too came to the room pretending I didn't know what was going on and together we handed out a few 'rollickings' for the mess and noise.

Once the boss was mollified I quickly sought out the men involved who were quite prepared to start all over again with the blonde in another room. This time there was no hesitation and the girl was politely but firmly ejected from the station. I subsequently found out she was a 'regular' on the station and in fact on all four watches! She also entertained half the household cavalry regiment stationed in Knightsbridge as well the Military Police stationed just down the road from us!!! Obviously a very popular girl!! She actually worked just down the road from the fire station and often she would stand on the island in the middle of the road to perform her 'Marilyn Monroe' moment. The underground subway ran down the middle of Euston road and when a train rushed through there would be a blast of air up through the grating and her skirt would be blown high revealing whatever she was wearing, or not wearing. This 'entertainment' wasn't just for the Firemen but the hundreds of commuters as well. It takes all sorts, I suppose!

This fire was just around the corner from the Fire station. We had been smelling smoke and seen it wafting across the sky for some time but thought it was probably a fire on a building site or something like that. As the Euston area is always busy with people it simply didn't cross anyone's mind on the Fire station that there could be a serious fire in progress! In fact it was a small engineering firm that was burning merrily away!! Someone eventually saw it and called us. That's me doing my 'I'm in charge bit'!

Receiving my Long Service and good conduct medal from the Chief Officer at a ceremony in County Hall. I initially refused to accept the medal as I was still very angry at being kicked out of the Training School on a 'trumped up' charge of insubordination, which was simply a personality thing with a senior officer. I figured that as I had been 'insubordinate' then how can I receive a 'good conduct' medal. I was told that receiving the medal was mandatory and it didn't matter if I was 'Jack the Ripper'! It would have been posted to me had I not gone to the ceremony; Having made my point I gave in gracefully!

ALL SORTS

Whilst there are many stories that can stand alone there are literally hundreds more that merit just a few lines but are equally funny in their own right, if you have that particular sense of humour of course!

For instance: We were called to a fire in Bayswater one afternoon. The whole of the station turned out as Bayswater is a high fire risk area and not only the three appliances from Kensington were sent but also another from Paddington. As we pulled into Porchester Terrace it was quite obvious there was a serious fire in one of the bedsits.

Speed is of the utmost essence where fire is concerned, for obvious reasons, and when the appliance I was riding pulled up I leapt off the machine and grabbed the ready use hose reel and ran towards the front door which was shut, pulling the hose as I ran. When I reached the door and without breaking stride I simply kicked at the door. I'm a big man and our fire boots are very useful tools for opening doors in a hurry! I had kicked very hard as I didn't want to spend time repeating the kick and the door flew off its hinges completely and crashed down into the hallway.

What I didn't know, but found out later, was that someone on another floor in the bedsit had seen us coming down the terrace, blue lights flashing and sirens sounding, and realising there was a fire on a floor above and so ran down the stairs to open the door to let us in. It was just his luck that as he arrived at the door to open it, I arrived like some rampaging buffalo on the other side and kicked it in.

It shows how much momentum I had that, as the door crashed into the hallway, I didn't realise at all that this poor man had received the door full in his face and was trapped under it as I stamped over and carried on up the stairs. The following crew discovered this poor chap and removed the door to help him out. I had clattered the poor bugger so hard he had to have hospital treatment. The fire was just another run of the mill job for us but the door kicking incident raised a few laughs around the mess table.

- - - - -

A rather sad incident, though in its own twisted way a funny occurrence, was at another fire in a house in Ladbrook Grove, North Kensington. It wasn't a particularly big fire though no doubt the occupier thought it big enough. It was the usual bed sit property though this time it was a very old lady who was the occupier and not the usual student or itinerant.

When we arrived, the old lady was standing outside and quite obviously distressed. It wasn't so much that her bedsit was alight, rather it was her pet budgerigar she was very concerned about. It is always part of our job to comfort people where possible, and though we were quite used to the stress and upset of these situations the average person isn't. She was assured that the very first thing we would do would be to bring the budgerigar out to her.

The fire wasn't a particularly fierce fire though as is common huge volumes of smoke were generated. The fire was dealt with and once relative safety was attained, the search for the budgie took place. Now, I'm afraid animals and particularly budgies do not fare well in an environment that will kill the average human being so there really wasn't much hope at all for this particular bird.

Sure enough there was the budgie lying on the bottom of its cage stone dead. John Cleese would probably have put it better!!

A quick chat amongst ourselves as to what to tell the old lady as she was very agitated and upset at the thought her budgie being in danger. One of the Firemen took it upon himself to sneak out with the cage without the woman seeing him.

He reached in and took the dead bird out and put it in his pocket then went to the woman with the empty cage, though with the door to the cage open. He explained that he had found the cage and the budgie was alive and well but looked somewhat dirty and unhappy! He said that he had opened the cage door to pet the bird but somehow it had escaped and had flown up into the trees! He went on to say that he had seen the bird in the trees and it seemed to be very happy and content though wouldn't return to the cage. The woman, though not a hundred percent happy that her bird had been lost by the Fire Brigade, did resign herself to losing the bird even if it was now alive and enjoying its freedom.

She obviously preferred that the bird was free and eventually was mollified enough to thank us for rescuing the budgie. The budgie, of course, ended up in the nearest dustbin.

- - - - -

Given almost any situation and Fireman will make the most of it in the most comic of ways. Fortunately the public very rarely get to see any of the childish behavior or I'm sure the Brigade would have to set up its own complaints department to deal with the flood of complaints that would surely follow if these comic situations were seen.

We were called to a patisserie in Westbourne Avenue one Saturday afternoon. I was still a Fireman at Kensington and we were ordered to the fire to assist Paddington. The fire wasn't a particularly bad fire though it was severe enough to warrant half a dozen appliances. As usual the biggest problem was smoke. The whole of the building was completely smoke logged with the fire lurking somewhere on one of the floors.

As is the practice of the Fire Service, search and rescue is always a priority, whilst at the same time the fire is attacked. I was part of the search crew and as such were given what amounts to free rein to search anywhere though obviously the search would always commence where people would most likely be trapped. As it was a commercial property, it was reasonable to assume that the work place would be the best place to start searching and that is where we started, in the patisserie making part.

The work place, in this case, was a large room with several huge tables on which were stacked and positioned dozens of cakes and other patisseries of every description from wedding cakes to doughnuts, many with seemingly gallons of cream oozing out from between layers of sponge and fruit cake. I would hasten to add at this point that due to the heavy smoke logging all of these cakes were now ruined, though that doesn't really excuse what followed.

It just happened that as our search team entered this room from one end so a search team from Paddington entered at the other. One of their search crew was, coincidentally, an old childhood mate who hailed from the same council estate. I don't know if our backgrounds were to blame but we certainly had the same sort of behavioral traits and as the two teams closed on each other, Dave, the leader of the other team, slapped down hard on a large and very creamy sponge cake and splattered us all in cream!

It took but a split second for retaliation to take place and cakes of all descriptions were being hurled around and it wasn't long before everyone was covered in cream and cake, an absolute mess. The whole room looked as if a group of maniacs had been let loose and some might say that was the case!

It wasn't too long before an officer arrived and saw what was going on when it was stopped and rollickings were handed out to all present. Given that we were standing there covered in cream, jam and cake it was difficult to deny what had happened. It took some disguising but eventually to get the place looking as if it had been involved in the fire and with some judicial placing of upturned tables etc. it seemed that the 'cake fight' was just part of the firefighting operations. I'm sure that if the owners of the shop had known what had gone on there would have been hell to pay!!! I do repeat though that all of the confectionery was ruined by smoke before we started playing silly buggers; no excuse I know and it isn't meant to be one.

- - - - -

Fire Stations are a magnet for every nutter walking the streets. Maybe these people can see in the Firemen some sort of kindred spirit!! Chelsea Fire station was situated absolutely perfectly for viewing and, sometimes 'entertaining' these people. The station is in the Kings Road, which is the heart of Chelsea. I enjoyed being stationed there on a temporary basis from time to time as watching all the 'beautiful people' parading themselves was quite something. Often personalities would pass by and tap on the window, Bruce Forsyth and Harry Secombe passed by one day and gave us a wave, at least Secombe did, Forsyth was far too snobbish.

Given its location and the numbers of people who walked by it was little wonder that from time to time Firemen would chat up some of the more 'receptive' types! On one occasion a couple of the men went 'missing' which was unusual as a Fire watch is a close-knit thing and usually the whole watch is gathered together, either playing sport or watching TV etc. So a couple missing was unusual.

It didn't take long to track them down and they were found in the basement with a couple of girls who were actively engaged in giving oral sex! Except they weren't girls. It turned out these 'girls' had more or less thrown themselves at the two Firemen and of course being loose, free and single themselves thought, why not and sneaked them into the station.

Once down in the basement the fun commenced but it was not long before it was discovered these two girls were boys. By the time this was discovered the foreplay was at an advanced stage and passions as well as other things were very much raised!! Sod it they thought and went ahead with the oral sex and according to their account afterwards, was very nice indeed. I knew the two men very well and they were definitely not of any persuasion other than normal but they simply said it was a question somewhat like, shut your eyes and think of England, only better! God knows what else went on at Chelsea but I bet that little episode was but a mere drop in the ocean.

- - - - -

There are all sorts of characters and personalities that go to making up a watch. I suppose the work attracts the outward types though not all, by any means, are extrovert. I have served on a watch where men have served in the Army, Navy and Air Force as well as from the Merchant Marine. Some had even left the Brigade and returned later having missed the service.

One such person on my watch at Paddington was certainly not extrovert. In fact he was the absolute complete opposite. Being very quiet and keeping to himself didn't exactly endear him to the other Firemen and in fact most disliked him. Being a junior officer I didn't have close contact with him. My job was mainly taking drill and giving lectures, but there was always something a little disconcerting about this particular man and difficult to put the proverbial finger on.

He had only been with us for about a year, having completed his initial training and then posted to us. His home address was in Northampton and he used to come down to London for his two-day shifts then go home returning the following day for his two-night shifts and again return to Northampton.

Apart from thinking he was a little strange that he should live so far away and commute all those miles no one really gave it much attention. He, himself, never commented on it and in fact rarely commented on anything. In the end he was just left to himself and never made any close association with anyone.

It was when he failed to turn up for duty one night that a deeper interest was taken in him. When someone doesn't turn up for duty it is the responsibility of the Officer in Charge to do some fundamental searching as the absentee may have had an accident or be ill. In his case he didn't have a home telephone and in the early hours of his non-showing it was felt too soon to ask the local Fire Brigade to go to his address and see if he was there.

It was whilst we were waiting for a suitable passage of time to pass before we contacted the local brigade, that the Northampton Police contacted us and the whole story came out. Quite a story as it turned out and we realized why this man used to keep himself to himself.

He was a career criminal! He was part of an organised car thieving gang based in Northampton and his role in this little enterprise was to come down to London and whilst here select a car to be stolen and then drive it back to Northampton where it would be either cannibalised or sold on, usually abroad.

What better cover than to be a Fireman! He would spend the first evening 'casing' a car, then the second evening simply steal it and drive home, or at least to wherever he dropped the cars off in Northampton. He would do the same on his night shift as well and in the year with us he must have stolen perhaps hundreds of cars. The Police had actually been tracking him for some time but didn't want to arrest him until they had all of the gang identified. They did have the grace to say that at one time they thought there were several Fireman involved but eventually realised he was working alone.

- - - - -

Fire appliances often featured in bizarre situations. We were called to a fire in the West End and I was riding the second Fire appliance in line. As we hurtled down Oxford St. my driver although excellent, did tend to become a little excited at times and as a consequence we were always within several feet of the rear end of the other appliance. I think it should be said that when travelling in convoy like this the second appliance driver relies somewhat on the first appliance driver 'clearing the road' in front and so driving so close isn't as dangerous as it sounds, most of the time.

On this occasion it didn't work! It was a Saturday afternoon and Oxford St was jammed pack with buses, taxis and the odd delivery lorry. We were probably doing around 30-40 mph and within about six feet of the rear of the appliance in front. Suddenly the brake lights of the appliance in front came on and the appliance in front seemed to launch itself at us! My driver stated afterwards that he just was checking his mirror at that precise moment and so was a second slow in reacting. Of course I believed him.

The appliance in front was carrying a ladder known as a '135' and this particular ladder extends to about three feet or so beyond the back of the appliance. As we braked heavily it avoided us slamming into the appliance in front but not enough to stop the rear end of this large metal ladder crashing through the windscreen and pinning me to the back of my seat.

Had the ladder come back as little as a few inches more I would have suffered very serious injuries and maybe even been killed. It was that close. As it was, I was pinned like a fly in my seat surrounded by glass and wreckage. There was blood dripping from several cuts to my hands which I had put up as the windscreen came in but which were now also pinned under the ladder. I didn't seem to be in any serious pain so didn't start screaming or shouting. That would have been most unseemly for the O.I.C. to do.

I couldn't do anything other than sit there and wait for my crew to rescue me. I also expected to see the crew from the other appliance come back and help out but to my utter amazement not only did they not appear but the appliance drove off! The ladder, which was pinning me to my seat was dragged off their machine as they drove away, the end crashing down into the road. My crew, having recovered from being thrown all over the place in the back when we struck, set about releasing me.

Now this being Oxford St in the middle of a Saturday afternoon there were thousands of people around all gawking at this added West End spectacle but when a Police motorcyclist appeared and stood in front of the appliance with a camera saying "this will look great on the canteen wall" and started taking snaps, I thought that wasn't really what he should be doing! Eventually the ladder was removed from my lap and I was able to look at my hands which were still bleeding heavily. After picking out several bits of glass and washing them I decided that first aid would suffice and set about trying to sort out something from all the confusion.

First I had to inform control that we couldn't attend the fire because of the accident (they would send a replacement). I then also asked control to inform the other appliance that they had a piece of equipment missing and would they come and collect it. This message was heavy on the sarcasm as I was still feeling pretty pissed off that they never helped after the accident.

They did come back to Oxford St about 30 minutes later. The call had been a false alarm! By way of explanation the O.I.C. of the appliance said that in all honesty they hadn't known there had been an accident and that was why they had carried on to the call. Given that we hadn't run into the back of their machine (the ladder didn't count!) I had to accept the explanation. He did have the grace to say though that he was somewhat surprised when control ordered him back to Oxford and he realized he had a huge metal ladder missing!

- - - - -

There have been many accidents involving fire appliances and that was just one of several bizarre ones I was involved with. One was the turntable ladder, a huge monster of a machine that could extend a ladder a hundred feet into the sky. We were called to a fire in Paddington and the turntable ladder and our pump were ordered to attend. The route we took was, from Kensington to Bayswater Road and then down Queensway. Halfway down and doing considerable speed with the turntable in front we were just crossing a junction with the traffic lights at green when a car jumped the red light coming from the right. The turntable ladder driver miraculously avoided the car by swerving but in doing so the immense weight of the vehicle took charge and broadsided across the junction, struck the pavement and to our incredulity flipped over on to its side and continued sliding down the pavement. This vehicle is approximately 30 ft long and weighs several ton. The real miracle of this accident was that not a single person was injured, let alone killed.

The second accident of note, though I wasn't there when it happened, but was ordered to attend the actual incident, was a collision between a double decker London Transport bus and an appliance from Chelsea fire station. Chelsea's pump was ordered to a fire in Kensington and on route used Queensgate as the most direct way to the call. This time it was the brigade's unequivocal fault the accident occurred. The fire appliance passed through a red traffic light just as the bus crossed the junction.

What happened next was straight out of a Buster Keaton film! The fire appliance struck the bus on the side but near the back. The force was such that the driver of the fire appliance was thrown out of the cab and the appliance continued on its merry way with the O.I.C. and crew wondering if they are going to get away without being killed! A short way further the appliance did come to a stop but used some parked cars to help it to do so.

Meanwhile the bus, because of its own momentum and being struck near the back, had broadsided across the junction and skidded up to the kerb, which acted as some kind of fulcrum, and the bus promptly tipped over on to its side crashing down on to the pavement. Again it was tantamount to a miracle that no one was injured, let alone killed. The bus had several passengers and not one was injured, shaken yes, and neither were any of the fire crew including the driver. Equally fortunate was that no one on the pavement was struck by the falling bus.

The chaos and wreckage when I arrived was quite incredible and it was in talking to the crew that I obtained all the details. The jokes, of course, went the rounds for weeks about knocking over a bus and driverless fire appliances. The driver of the appliance was relieved from driving, something he had been trying to achieve for a year or so! It makes you wonder.

- - - - -

The practical jokes that occur on Fire stations are, or were, regarded as simply being part of life on the station. When I joined in 1965 the shift system I was on meant I did two day duties of nine hours a day followed by two night duties of fifteen hours each night. Then followed two days rest, the first being from when you finished the second night shift plus one additional day. The whole cycle would then be repeated ad infinitum, a 56 hour week.

Drills and lectures form part of the everyday life of a Fireman but there is only so much drilling and lectures to be done, particularly on a long night shift and that was usually the time for pranksters to get going. Going to the toilet you would think was a safe and perfectly normal human function but often it resulted in a bucket of water coming through a carelessly left open window. I well remember two occasions when a 'prank' almost ended in disaster! On both occasions a member of the watch was locked in a small room used for storage and burning newspapers were lobbed in through a small window.

What we didn't appreciate was that there were flammable mattresses stored in there and they were catching alight quicker than the poor unfortunate could put them out. It wasn't until it became very quiet and smoke began creeping out beneath the door that we opened up to find the fireman semi-conscious on the floor and quite a respectable fire burning! Had we kept the door shut much longer, I shudder to think what would have happened, all in the name of fun.

The list of pranks is almost endless: forcing a Fireman to run across Euston Road naked on his birthday, tying up and suspending men from the training tower, jacking up a Fireman's car so the drive wheels are just clear of the ground. When he tries to drive he thinks perhaps the clutch has broken!! There really was no end to what the personnel would or could get up to. I have been retired now for almost as long as I served and I still miss the life I led back then. I learned many valuable lessons from men which stood me in good stead for the rest of my life. They had seen it and done it, unlike me who at 18 years of age thought I knew everything.

- - - - -

One very fortuitous event happened in the Portland Hospital, Great Portland St. I say fortuitous because had what followed happened elsewhere I may well have had a dead body on my hands!!

We had been called to someone shut in a lift in the hospital. This was an everyday occurrence and during every shift it was normal to receive a call like this. Because we attended so many of these calls the procedure was automatic. A couple of Firemen would go to the lift motor room whilst I found the floor or between floors where the lift had stopped.

I would open up a door above where the lift was jammed using a special key and peer into the shaft. Once located I would call up through the shaft to the men in the motor room to wind the lift, by hand, up to me. I say up because the counterweight of the lift made that the easiest direction to move a lift by hand. The Firemen in the motor room knew exactly what I wanted and started to wind the lift up whilst

I waited at the opened door. Now, often we had hand held radios to use in situations like this but just as often the bloody things didn't work! That meant when the lift drew parallel with me I would need to shout very loudly into the lift so that the Firemen up top would stop winding.

As the interior of the lift came into view I saw two elderly women standing there looking somewhat concerned. I talked to them and said everything is under control and to wait until I tell them to leave the lift. That was necessary because it has been known for a disabled lift to suddenly be 'abled' and shoot off trapping someone trying to exit the lift before being told to do so; resulting in serious injury.

The lift drew level and I bellowed "WELL" into the lift 'well' being Fireman terminology for 'STOP'. It was necessary to shout loud as the men doing the winding in the lift motor room had to stop winding and secure the lift. Unfortunately I had neglected to inform the two elderly ladies about this and they were both extremely startled to suddenly have this huge Fireman bawling like an Army Sergeant Major about two feet from their faces.

The result was that one of them promptly collapsed and the other staggered backwards. Now we come to the fortuitous part of the story. Fortuitous because there we all were in probably the very best private hospital in the country which cares for the rich, famous and of course Royalty. Hospital staff immediately took over and whisked the two ladies away to no doubt receive the very best medical attention money can buy, though no doubt, because of the circumstances this treatment was free!!

It transpired that the lady who had collapsed had just fainted and recovered quickly. The other lady was perfectly fine and in fact they both, so I was informed, saw the funny side of it. Much to my relief actually as I could see all sorts of complications arising from my actions, albeit innocent ones.

- - - - -

As these stories have, in the main, been about other Fireman falling prey to practical jokes I suppose I should finish with a story that the expression 'hoist by his own petard' fits perfectly. I was detailed to be the watchroom attendant on a night duty. As has been explained earlier it meant that I would be sitting down stairs in my watchroom unable to get any 'shuteye' until well after midnight.

The reason for that was that the logbook had to be dated and signed with the start of a new day at 00.01. So, there I sat and my fertile mind got to thinking of something I could do to make the night entertaining. By that I mean get up to some mischief! The rest of the watch had 'turned in' and the station was as quite as a cemetery.

Pulling any sort of stunt can be a little dangerous! Firemen tended to get a bit grumpy if their 'kip' is disturbed and I didn't want to end up on the end of someone's bad temper! But what to do, I just couldn't let an opportunity go by; after all I had a reputation to consider!

We had, in the basement, a dummy which was used for some of the more dangerous drills we carried out. An ugly looking thing which was the weight of an average person; around 12 stone or 170 pounds. It had the usual two arms and legs and was made of heavy duty canvas. The face was simply a plain round affair and totally without expression which gave it a very creepy sort of look. An idea formed in my mind as to how I could use this dummy to surprise the rest of the watch.

Ensuring that everyone had turned in and that I wouldn't be disturbed I crept down into the basement and retrieved the dummy from the store room. Hoisting it on to my back I climbed the several flights of stairs to the first floor. Had anyone seen me they would probably have done a double take! I must have looked like some sort of body snatcher carrying his victim somewhere; which in a way I was!

Most of the men slept in the locker room on the first floor and this was accessed from a small lobby from the stairs. A door separating the two. Creeping into the lobby I found a suitable fixing point to hang the dummy by a rope around its neck and left in hanging outside the door to the locker room.

The idea was anyone coming out of the locker would jump out of their skin being confronted by an apparently dead body hanging by its neck! Having sissified myself all was well I quietly retired to my watchroom. Kensington, being a busy station, would no doubt have a call during the night and the Firemen rushing out of the locker room in answer to 'the bells' would have a fright; it was simply a matter of time.

The night wore on and having completed all my duties I thought I would just lie down and doze a bit waiting for a fire call to come in. Part of the unofficial duty of the watchroom attendant was to make tea for the rest of the watch in the morning. The dutyman was always the first to be up and about as there were further bookings and things to do. Once these things were attended to it was off to the kitchen to make a big pot of tea and loaded with cups, sugar, etc.; serve to everyone in bed; all very civilised!

The morning duly arrived and having had not a single call I finished my work and went off to make the tea. Loaded down as I was with a large tray filled with cups my first stop was to the locker room. Not having had a call all night and then having to do whatever was necessary in the watchroom I had completely forgotten about the 'dead body' hanging in the lobby.

The station was still in semi darkness and absolutely silent as I turned the corner into the lobby to be confronted by the apparition hanging by its neck! The surprise was such that I'm sure I must have jumped clear off the ground. The tray not being as jumpy as I was didn't follow my maneuver and flew out of my hands crashing down on to the floor with a tremendous crash. Everything was broken and tea, of course, everywhere. The noise would have woken the dead and sure enough the door opened and several Firemen stood staring regarding; first me, then the dummy and finally the mess on the floor.

Everyone was, of course, well pleased with the outcome, except me. I suppose it further cemented my relationship with the others though as they did see the funny side of it and they were never short of pulling tricks of their own. I never did try that one again though; I'm not sure we had enough crockery!

This book has been about the practical jokes, some, no doubt, absolutely childish, maybe all of them but that is for the reader to decide. For me it was part of the 'job'. The other, serious side of the Fire service has been written about countless times and I simply couldn't write about that side as well as most. I have been to enough funerals of Firemen killed on duty to know what the 'job' can take from its members. With that in mind perhaps any reader will allow for the behavior of these men, when they are not rushing into harm's way.

Printed in Great Britain
by Amazon